A kitchen is never just a kitchen—it's a place where memories are not only created but also stored and treasured.

ENCHANTED KITCHEN

GAIL BUSSI

first discovered green magic as a little girl in her mother's flower garden. After some years spent writing, designing, and working as a professional cook, she decided to return to her first love and obtained qualifications in holistic herbalism, flower therapies, and mindfulness coaching. Today she lives in a small log cabin on the beautiful Eastern Cape coast of South Africa, where she continues to write, teach, and create natural enchantment every day.

AUTHOR OF
Enchanted Herbal
Gail Bussi

ENCHANTED KITCHEN

Connect *to* Spirit with
Recipes & Rituals
Through the
Year

Llewellyn Publications
WOODBURY, MINNESOTA

FIRST EDITION
Second Printing, 2023

Book design by Rebecca Zins
Cover design by Shira Atakpu

Llewellyn is a registered trademark of Llewellyn Worldwide Ltd.

Library of Congress Cataloging-In-Publication Data
Names: Bussi, Gail, author.
Title: Enchanted kitchen : connect to spirit with recipes & rituals through the year / Gail Bussi.
Description: First edition. | Woodbury, Minnesota : Llewellyn Publications, [2022] | Includes bibliographical references. | Summary: "Part guidebook, part recipe book, and part inspirational journey, *Enchanted Kitchen* is about the stories, magic, food, and traditions specific to each month and the nourishment for the body, heart, and soul that begins in our kitchens"—Provided by publisher.
Identifiers: LCCN 2022006471 (print) | LCCN 2022006472 (ebook) | ISBN 9780738770604 (paperback) | ISBN 9780738770659 (ebook)
Subjects: LCSH: Seasonal cooking. | Magic. | LCGFT: Cookbooks.
Classification: LCC TX714 .B883 2022 (print) | LCC TX714 (ebook) | DDC 641.5/64—dc23/eng/20220214
LC record available at https://lccn.loc.gov/2022006471
LC ebook record available at https://lccn.loc.gov/2022006472

Llewellyn Worldwide Ltd. does not participate in, endorse, or have any authority or responsibility concerning private business transactions between our authors and the public.

All mail addressed to the author is forwarded but the publisher cannot, unless specifically instructed by the author, give out an address or phone number.

Any internet references contained in this work are current at publication time, but the publisher cannot guarantee that a specific location will continue to be maintained. Please refer to the publisher's website for links to authors' websites and other sources.

Llewellyn Publications
A Division of Llewellyn Worldwide Ltd.
2143 Wooddale Drive
Woodbury, MN 55125-2989
www.llewellyn.com
Printed in the United States of America

This book is lovingly dedicated to all of those who have shared my kitchen journey, both past and present. We have laughed, shared, and cooked together in these precious moments. And it's especially dedicated to my mother, Catharine. I know we will cook together again one day in the lands of light and joy.

CONTENTS

CONTENTS

RECIPES

Edible Magic

Everyday Magic

Food is just something you grow and recipes are just words written in notebooks. They are nothing until the right person comes along. And that's when the real magic happens.

Sarah Addison Allen

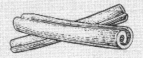

INTRODUCTION

What is kitchen magic? What does it mean to be a kitchen witch? For starters, it's a powerful source of enchantment that is available to everybody, no matter who we are, where we live, and what our personal circumstances may be. I've known people living in extremely difficult circumstances who still made their kitchens, however small and humble, places of joy and welcome for all who came there.

What is the difference between a kitchen and a hearth witch (for the term is often used interchangeably)? In many ways they are the same, since the term "hearth" originally denoted the kitchen and center of the home; in simple terms, a kitchen witch is someone, male or female, who uses the simple everyday kitchen activities of cooking

and baking as a way of seeing and creating the magic that is inherent in even the most basic of our everyday actions. We see kitchens as a place of active involvement in the creation of joy, healing, and enchantment, both for ourselves and those we hold dear—family, friends, pets, and the greater community around us.

Green or hedge witches follow similar paths but are often also more actively engaged in the garden aspects of magic and in herbalism in general. For the purpose of this book, I am going to use the term "kitchen witch"— one who generally follows the simple magic path in both kitchen and home.

If we consider it, the regular preparation and consumption of food is pretty much essential to maintaining life and health. As it forms a significant part of the structure of our daily lives, why not make it a joyful and spiritual thing on a deeper level instead of just heating up canned soup or making toast? I know that sometimes we can see our daily tasks in the kitchen as being a necessary evil at best or totally boring at worst, but I hope this book will help us all see our kitchen in a new and more magical light as a place we actually enjoy and cherish every day.

A while ago, after starting to follow my own green and intuitive path (which resulted in my studies of herbalism

and other natural therapies, as well as the writing of my first book, *Enchanted Herbal*), I found myself being drawn back into the kitchen on a different and deeper level. I had been an avid cook and baker for much of my life and had worked professionally for a while in this field, but I had let that go for a while as a result of some fairly major shifts and changes in my life over a few years that I needed to work through on many levels.

Obviously I was already aware of the power and possibilities inherent in herbs, flowers, and other plants because of my studies and writing, but strangely it took me a little while longer to cotton on to the fact that my everyday cooking (in a fairly small and unremarkable kitchen) was also imbued with wonderful magical properties to bless heart, body, and soul.

After all, everything we eat is part of the earth—it grows on it, walks on it, or swims in the waters that cover so much of our planet—and if it's not part of the earth, we probably shouldn't be eating it! We are not separate from the food we eat, which is something ancient traditions and cultures knew so well. They respected the food they grew or gathered, and considered all foods to have their own particular magic, power, and meaning. Even something as simple as salt, which we all pretty much take for granted these days,

has been used for centuries across different cultures and beliefs for its powerful protective and healing qualities.

And, of course, the wheel of our year, with the turning and changing seasons, is also a vital part of our lives, one in which we can and should celebrate the sacred and ordinary joys that each season brings. I created this book to be part guidebook, part recipe book, and part inspirational journey for each of us who wants to see and experience our kitchens and cooking—whether we do it for ourselves, our loved ones, or the greater community around us—as a spiritual and personal practice that nourishes not only bodies but also hearts and souls.

And I hope the book is fun too—with ideas for rituals, self-care, health practices, meditations, and more!

I am aware that for some people, particularly women, the kitchen can seem to be a place of drudgery, a place of "have to" rather than "want to"; my mother was the classic example of this. I remember her being a very creative cook when I was young, always planning special meals and entertaining. It was only much later, toward the end of her life, that she confessed to me she often hated being in the kitchen and having to prepare meals, but she felt that, as a wife and mother, she had no choice. I found this sad but understandable. And if this feeling resonates with you, I hope this book will help change your mind and shift your

ideas about kitchens from places of boring routine and duty to places of enchantment and joy.

I love this quote by Roald Dahl: "A little magic can take you a long way"—it seems to me to sum up the very essence of this book by reminding us all that there is simple magic, healing, and joy to be found in the ordinary, every-day things we may sometimes take for granted—and never more so than in the food we prepare, eat, and share.

Kitchen enchantment is all about choice—and it starts with seeing our kitchens in a new light and turning them into a truly nourishing and nurturing heart of the home. Being a kitchen witch (and by using that term I certainly do not exclude men from this delicious role) is something we can all do and be—starting today. Enjoy your year of kitchen witchery. Celebrate each month and moment of this precious and enchanted life!

Excellence does not
require perfection.

Henry James

A Few Notes About This Book

- It was written for North American readers, with relevant measurements, food terms, and more; however, lists of food equivalents, kitchen measurements, and some ingredient names are given in the appendix for readers from other parts of the world.

- If a particular ingredient is unavailable or unsuitable (because of allergies, personal taste, etc.), just leave it out. Where possible I give alternatives in recipes; for example, for those who prefer not to cook with alcohol. In general I use fairly simple and easily obtainable ingredients; the same applies to the herbs and spices used in recipes, as I am presupposing that readers of this book will have a basic selection of fresh and dried herbs or spices at their disposal. Please always ensure that the herbs, spices, and flowers you use in your recipes are not chemically treated in any way and use organic when possible. Use herbs fresh or dried; if fresh, make sure they are finely

chopped, and if dried, use one-third the amount of fresh (so 1 tablespoon fresh = 1 teaspoon dried).

◆ This is not a vegetarian cookbook, and some of the recipes do include meat, chicken, and fish. However, in many instances, it is possible to adapt the recipe for vegetarian and vegan people. Ideas for this are given in the recipes.

◆ Hopefully we are all becoming more aware in our food choices—buying green, buying local, and choosing ethically raised meat or poultry and sustainable fish. If you honor life in all its forms, please make a point of buying only meat that has been raised in an organic and totally humane way! Magic in the kitchen starts with earth-conscious choices on every level. It's even more magical if you can grow at least some of your food yourself.

◆ This book is divided into the twelve months of the year, with stories, recipes, and traditions particular to each month; however, you can dip into it as and where you choose and simply enjoy

a magical kitchen journey wherever in the year we happen to be. Kitchen witchery should be both flexible and fun!

- There is a special section in each month devoted to the magic pantry—this is a very important part of kitchen enchantment as far as I am concerned, as any kitchen witch worth their salt (pardon the pun!) should have a pantry or even just a shelf devoted to magical potions, condiments, preserves, and more. This is such a delightful part of the whole kitchen witch tradition, but to me it's more than that: it's a way of honoring the cycles of the earth and her bounty. When we harvest, bottle, store, and preserve the gifts we receive from Mother Earth, we connect in a deeper and more meaningful way to this enchanted cycle of life—far more so than simply going to the store and buying a bottle of flavored salt or tomato ketchup.

- I am going to suggest keeping a kitchen journal if you don't already do so. It can simply be a record of recipes, meal ideas, and so on, but it can also be so much more. I love that there are

kitchen journals available now that include space for personal thoughts, memories, and so on, but of course you can simply use blank notebooks of your choice and make your kitchen journal entirely personal and unique. It's a lot of fun!

◆ Although this particular book follows the traditional Celtic wheel of the year in general, I must emphasize that this is not prescriptive in any way! There are so many different ways of celebrating and following the natural and magical path of kitchen witchery. I encourage you to make this book your own by simply using it as a stepping-stone to your own individual enchanted journey, both in the kitchen and beyond.

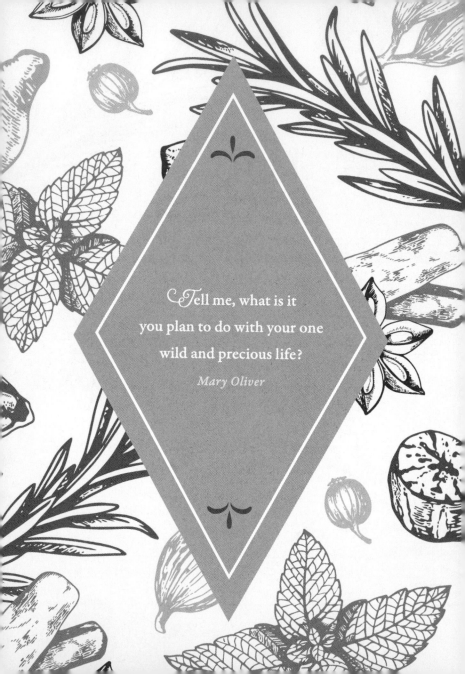

Tell me, what is it
you plan to do with your one
wild and precious life?

Mary Oliver

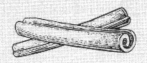

JANUARY

Nourish and Nurture

This quote from Mary Oliver seems particularly appropriate at the beginning of a new year, a fresh start with new horizons, challenges, and moments of magic. Our lives are indeed both wild and precious, and never more so than in what would sometimes otherwise be considered the ordinary moments and rituals of our everyday lives.

In January we stand on the very threshold of the year, with all its as-yet-unknown blessings, challenges, and opportunities. The celebrations of the holidays are behind us, and we look forward with hope and (sometimes) a little trepidation to the future. It's cold, too, if we live in the northern hemisphere, and often we are depleted physically by winter ailments like colds, coughs, and flu. Many of us, myself included, find January a difficult month in many ways, and that's why it's particularly important to focus on both nourishment and nurture for body and soul at this time.

Outside it may be chilly, with freezing winds and darkness falling quickly and early, but inside the January kitchen we should find a haven of comfort, warmth, and nourishment, as people have been doing for centuries and through all traditions and beliefs—a place where we can rest and dream and give ourselves space to become both peaceful and fully ourselves while outside icy winds blow. This is the time for simple nurturing of both ourselves and those we love, and what better way than by preparing and enjoying uplifting and soothing foods, recipes that nourish both body and soul, the very definition of comfort food and indeed of hearth witchery—the ancient art of keeping the home fires burning in the most true and practical of ways!

The January kitchen reminds us of where we came from, the warm womb of safety and belonging; the earth we dwell in, where we are and always have been, blessed in so many magical and unexpected ways.

In January we put the past year behind us and look to the future; this is the birth of a new cycle in the wheel of the year, and, like any birth, it can sometimes be painful and difficult but ultimately leads us on to new and beautiful things. Planting seeds in cold and sometimes seemingly barren earth, we wait with hope and faith for growth and blossoming to come.

The traditional kitchen goddess for this month—and indeed throughout the wheel of the year—is Hestia, Greek goddess of hearth, home, and hospitality. She lived on Mount Olympus, like the other great Greek deities, but unlike them she seems to have been a lot more down-to-earth and approachable. A beautiful woman, she was apparently sought after by both Apollo and Poseidon, who wanted to marry her, but she chose to remain as she was, in her own home and living for the joy of making others warm, welcome, and comfortable. It would appear Hestia was quite an interesting woman who had no truck with the "rules" governing women at that time!

In every ancient Greek home, the hearth was dedicated to Hestia and the fire was not allowed to go out; if a family moved, they would bring fire from the old hearth to light the new. The Romans also borrowed Hestia, whom they renamed Vesta, and she was similarly worshiped in homes and temples.

When we invite people into our home or simply share what we have with those around us—loved ones, friends, strangers, pets—we are invoking Hestia and her powerful generosity and warmth of spirit, something much needed in our world today. So, too, when we prepare and serve food that is warming, abundant, and life sustaining, we honor her and her comforting spirit. So let us remember Hestia and her many gifts to us not only in January but throughout our enchanted year!

The Blessing Candle

On the windowsill in my kitchen, I have a white pillar candle nestled upon an old blue china plate from Greece that is the color of the Aegean Sea. This is my kitchen blessing candle, and although I might light it a few times during the week, I make a point of always lighting it on a Sunday evening to remember and honor the week just passed and the week to come.

I started doing this some time ago while going through some difficult times that left me dispirited, anxious, and sad. One evening I walked into my kitchen and stopped for a moment. There was good food in the cupboards and fridge, there were lots of pretty dishes and glasses and saucepans, there were fragrant herbs in pots and a row of much-loved cookbooks on a shelf. I realized in that

moment how truly blessed I was, with abundance on both physical and emotional levels, and so I had been for most of my life. I had never known hunger or, indeed, any kind of lack in my life; I had been encouraged to spend time in the kitchen with my mother and aunts and friends, laughing, tasting, learning, and making delicious feasts.

And even though my mother and I, like so many mothers and daughters, had our conflicts, the kitchen remained the place where we could connect on a simple heart level—chopping and stirring, sharing recipes, and taking time to remember all the good we still shared. (Although she still always said I used too much garlic!) It was for all these reasons and more that I started my simple blessing candle ritual in my kitchen, a joyful practice for all us kitchen witches.

First, choose your candle, which should be fairly large and sturdy in shape (not a taper); I prefer using a white candle but again that's a matter of preference. My candle is also unscented, although I do occasionally add a few drops of essential oil to the melted pool of wax around the wick: something simple and calming like lavender, an old favorite, although rosemary, lemon, sweet orange, or vanilla also works well in a kitchen setting. This is a lovely ritual to do either alone or as a family or group.

Remove your shoes and stand with your feet a little apart. Breathe deeply and steadily for a few minutes. Make a conscious effort to drop your shoulders and feel your body releasing tension as your energy flows down into the grounding earth. Light your candle. After gazing into the flame for a few minutes, softly say these words:

We light this blessing candle to remember. We remember how blessed we are with abundance from the earth and her many gifts to us. We are blessed with memories of love given and received, of all good things we have known in our lives. We gather at the table in the kitchen, and the moment is both simple and sacred. We remember. We are blessed. And so it is.

The candle can be left burning for at least 15 to 20 minutes or longer if you prefer. Always remember to safely extinguish any lit candles.

Good Vibrations

It's something we've all experienced: we walk into a room and immediately feel a sense of unease and discomfort. There is a negative energy to the place that makes us anxious to leave as soon as possible. On the other hand, there are times when we enter a room that exudes a joyous and

peaceful sense of having come home, even if we have never been there before. We feel grounded, grateful, and simply happy to be there.

This isn't surprising when we consider that everything, and I do mean everything, has its own unique energy, a living force that makes it exactly what it is. Everything—from the ground we walk on to the plants we grow to the foods we eat and, of course, ourselves—has this amazing energy, which can be either positive or negative in nature.

As we come to the beginning of the new year, January is the perfect month to seek out positive and healing energies in both our surroundings and ourselves, and the kitchen is the perfect place to begin. It all starts with a (relatively) clean and orderly kitchen space. Obviously a kitchen doesn't have to be a totally sterile environment that resembles an operating theatre, but equally a dirty, chaotic, or overly cluttered kitchen is off-putting and stressful on every level of the senses. It also makes cooking more pleasant when we have an orderly space in which we can easily find and access ingredients, utensils, and other things we need without having to spend an hour rummaging through a crammed larder in search of an elusive bottle of ground paprika. (Ask me how I know this!)

If you find your kitchen energy is stagnant or tiring, making it a place you would frankly rather avoid if at all

possible, a valuable tool is to make a simple purifying mixture that can either be simmered on the stove top or decanted into a spray bottle once it is cold. Needless to say, this can be used at any time during the year.

Bring a pan of spring water to boil, then add a handful of sea salt, a lemon cut into halves or quarters (you can also use dried lemon peel), a few sprigs of rosemary, and a handful of pine needles or eucalyptus, if you can find them. Simmer gently for at least 30 minutes, allowing the fragrance to fill every corner of your kitchen, then cool and use in a spray bottle. This mixture is wonderful for protection and purification (sea salt and lemon), vitality and health (pine needles and eucalyptus), and positive thinking and energy (rosemary).

A Kitchen Spell Bottle

Kitchens need protection and clearing just like any other room in your home. This simple little spell bottle is fun to put together and can either be placed on a shelf or hung up with colorful ribbons or cords. (I keep mine suspended from a picture hook on the wall.) They also make delightful gifts, especially for people moving into new homes.

I like to use either blue or clear glass bottles that are not too large and preferably have cork tops. Sprinkle a little pink Himalayan salt in the bottom of the bottle (for pro-

tection and cleansing), then add the following: a sprig of lavender (peace), a dried bay leaf (courage), an amethyst crystal (peace and protection), and a small white feather to represent angel or goddess spirits.

Write the following on a small piece of paper (or you can use your own words):

My kitchen is a sacred place, a place of warmth,
a place of joy, sharing, and nourishment. May
it be blessed by Brigid and the Shining Ones,
and may all who gather in this place know
only peace and abundance. And so it is.

Roll up the paper into a scroll that will fit into the bottle and tie it with a thin white or purple ribbon. Lastly, sprinkle the scroll with a few drops of rose essential oil (for love and peace) and place the scroll in your prepared bottle.

Kitchen Pleasures

- Try to get up a little earlier in the morning (yes, I know it can be awful to leave a cozy bed in the dark winter cold) and spend some quiet time in your kitchen with a cup of your favorite hot drink. It's a good time to write in your kitchen (or other) journal; I also like to keep a couple of favorite small books of affirmations/thoughts with my cookbooks and often take one down to browse through it. It's amazing how frequently I find some thought or quote that seems particularly appropriate for that day.

- If possible, try to refrain from using your phone, tablet, or laptop too much in your kitchen. Kitchen mindfulness starts with focusing on ourselves and whatever it is we are doing in that moment—and phones, with their constant beeps, chirps, and messages, are definitely not helpful in that regard.

- Keep something green and growing in your kitchen as a reminder that, no matter how dark and cold it may be outside, life still continues in all its forms, and spring will return. Herbs in pots are the obvious choice: parsley, chives, sage, or thyme are all possibilities.

- Likely our kitchens have their own delicious aromas, but we can also use incense to add another dimension of magic. I particularly like sandalwood for kitchen use as it helps remove any negativity and promotes positive, happy vibes.

- To keep healthy boundaries in your kitchen throughout the year, mix a little crumbled lavender, dried rosemary, and pine needles with some sage and salt, and stir into a ½ cup cornstarch. Sprinkle a little of this mixture in the corners of your kitchen on a regular basis; it can be used in the other rooms of your home, too.

- In Middle European traditions, sprigs of basil were always hung up in the kitchen on January 6. Basil is an extremely powerful herb that dispels negative or harmful forces.

23

RECIPES

Moon Magic Soup

SERVES 4–6

This is a colorful, warming, uplifting soup with its roots in traditional Hungarian goulash. With both restorative and delicious qualities, it's the perfect soup for a cold and frosty night! Garlic and onion both have powerful medicinal qualities, especially when it comes to winter ailments like coughs and colds, while paprika, with its vibrant color, makes a wonderful creativity booster. (You can also use smoked paprika in this recipe, which adds a slightly different flavor dimension.) Tomatoes certainly warm the heart and lift the spirit, and in your garden or kitchen they will help keep negative energy (and malevolent entities) at bay.

> **4 tablespoons olive oil, divided**
> **2 onions, peeled and finely chopped**
> **2 garlic cloves, crushed**
> **1 red chili, chopped (optional)**
> **½ pound lean chuck steak**

2 cups canned tomatoes

2 tablespoons paprika

1 tablespoon tomato paste

4 cups beef broth

1 cup beer (optional)

1 teaspoon dried thyme

2 bay leaves

Salt and pepper

Chopped fresh parsley

Sour cream or natural yogurt

Warm 2 tablespoons of the oil in a large deep saucepan, and fry the onions, garlic, and chili until soft and transparent. Remove from the pan. Cut the steak into fairly small cubes (½ inch) and fry in 2 tablespoons oil until golden brown. Return the onion, garlic, and chili mixture to the pan. Add the tomatoes, paprika, and tomato paste. Stir in the broth and beer; if not using beer, add a little more broth or water. Add the dried herbs and salt and pepper to taste, then simmer for an hour or until the meat is soft and the soup has thickened slightly. Skim off any fat on the surface of the soup.

Serve piping hot, sprinkled with fresh parsley and topped with a spoon of sour cream or yogurt. It goes very well with good bread, too.

To adapt this for vegetarians: follow the recipe as given but replace the beef broth with vegetable broth and the meat with ½ pound of brown mushrooms that have been cut into fairly chunky pieces. The cooking time will be less than for the meat. If you leave off the sour cream or yogurt topping, you will have a delicious vegan dish.

Poor Man's Lasagne
SERVES 4–6

Despite the rather unfortunate name, this is a delicious and simple dish. I was given the recipe years ago by an Italian friend's mother, who told me she privately called it "Stretch the Month Dinner"—a good recipe for January, when many of us feel the pinch financially after holiday spending! It's made with ingredients that most of us have in our pantries or fridges, and if you don't have any homemade tomato sauce on hand (see recipe on page 200), you can simply substitute 2 cups canned tomato puree into which you have stirred a little crushed garlic, some dried oregano and basil, and some freshly ground black pepper.

The one essential in this recipe is fairly firm bread (of a sourdough or ciabatta type); it can even be a little hard or stale, as long as it's not moldy. Please don't use very soft white bread as it becomes too mushy and rather

unappetizing. As an alternative, you can use slices of peeled parboiled potato instead of the bread.

Preheat oven to 350°F. Butter a deep round or square casserole dish very well.

> **10–15 thin slices of bread**
>
> **Milk for dipping**
>
> **2½ cups tomato sauce**
>
> **1 tablespoon chopped fresh oregano or**
> **1 teaspoon dried oregano**
>
> **¾ pound mozzarella cheese**
>
> **4 eggs**
>
> **½ cup milk or light cream**
>
> **¼ cup grated Parmesan**

Assemble the dish as follows: dip 3 to 4 slices of bread into milk briefly, then arrange in the casserole dish, top with a thin layer of tomato sauce and sprinkle with a little oregano and a layer of grated or thinly sliced mozzarella cheese. You should have 3 or 4 layers, ending with tomato sauce and cheese. Beat the eggs very well with the milk or cream and pour evenly over the bread slices. Sprinkle with the grated Parmesan and bake for 50 minutes to an hour, or until the top of the dish has puffed up and is golden brown. Serve hot.

Chakalaka

MAKES ABOUT 3½ CUPS

What? Probably new to many, this is a South African township vegetable dish that is served warm or cold with just about anything! I think it makes the perfect January side dish because it uses vegetables freely available in the winter, as well as beans, which are often used in traditional cooking and magic at this time.

The chilies are essential, but you can control the heat by using less or removing the seeds. If you can't find baked beans in tomato sauce, simply use a can of ordinary butter or cannellini beans and add ½ cup tomato puree. Some people also add a small can of corn and/or some thinly sliced green beans to the chakalaka.

> ½ cup vegetable oil
>
> 1 large onion, chopped
>
> 2 green peppers, diced
>
> 2 green chilies, chopped
>
> 2 teaspoons curry powder
>
> 4 grated carrots
>
> 14-ounce can baked beans in tomato sauce
>
> ½ teaspoon hot sauce

Heat the oil to a medium heat in a large and fairly deep saucepan. Sauté the onion, peppers, and chilies until the onions are soft and translucent. Stir in the curry power, fry briefly, then add the carrots and simmer gently for about 20 minutes. Add the baked beans and hot sauce, and continue to cook for about 15 minutes or until the mixture is fairly thick.

Serve hot or cold. Stored in a covered glass dish or jar, chakalaka will keep well for at least 10 days in the fridge.

Upside-Down Orange and Almond Cake
SERVES 6–8

A bright gift from the sun for a chilly January day, oranges are traditionally linked with solar powers, bringing warmth, happiness, and positive energy on all levels. This cake is also suitable as a dessert and is particularly delicious served with heavy cream or Greek yogurt. You will need thin-skinned juicy oranges. I've also made this dish with blood oranges, which look particularly vibrant and colorful at this season.

If you don't have self-rising flour on hand, make your own with 1 cup all-purpose flour plus 1½ teaspoons baking powder and ¼ teaspoon salt.

Preheat oven to 350°F. Grease a deep 9-inch square baking pan very well.

1 cup superfine sugar

½ cup water

1 teaspoon vanilla extract

2–3 large oranges

4 eggs

1 cup sugar

1 teaspoon almond extract

1 cup self-rising flour, sifted

⅔ cup butter, melted

1 cup ground almonds

Place the superfine sugar, water, and vanilla extract in a saucepan and heat gently until the sugar has dissolved. Thinly slice the oranges, removing any pips, and simmer them in the syrup for 10 to 15 minutes. Remove from the heat and allow to cool. Strain the oranges and reserve the syrup for serving.

Beat the eggs, sugar, and almond essence in a large bowl until very light and fluffy, then gently fold in the flour. Stir in the melted butter and lastly add the ground almonds. Arrange the orange slices in a single layer in the prepared baking pan, then spoon the cake batter on top and spread evenly. Bake 45 minutes or until the cake is risen and tests done. Turn out onto a wire rack to cool and drizzle with a little of the remaining orange syrup.

Scottish Cheese Scones

MAKES 10–15 SCONES

Hogmanay, the Scottish New Year, is an occasion for much celebration and whiskey drinking on January 1. My great aunt Eileen got this recipe from her mother many moons ago, and her scones are certainly appropriate for any January feast, served warm with soups and stews or simply eaten out of hand with lots of butter. If you prefer a sweet scone, omit the cheese and add ¼ cup sugar. The thyme is my addition; it's a protective herb that brings us courage and confidence going forward, but it can also be omitted or replaced with another herb, like sage or chives.

> **2 cups flour, sifted**
> **1 tablespoon baking powder**
> **½ teaspoon salt**
> **1 cup grated Cheddar**
> **1 stick unsalted butter, chilled**
> **2 teaspoons dried or fresh thyme**
> **Ground paprika (optional)**
> **1 egg**
> **½ cup buttermilk**

Preheat oven to 400°F and grease a large baking or cookie sheet well.

Place the flour, baking powder, salt, and grated cheese in a large bowl. Grate the butter into the flour, then rub it

in lightly with your fingers until the mixture is like bread-crumbs. Stir in the herbs (if using). Beat the egg and but-termilk together in a cup, then pour into the flour mixture and mix to form a soft dough.

Pat out on a floured board or suitable surface; it's important not to handle the dough too much as that makes scones heavy and tough. The dough should be about ¾-inch thick. Cut out scones using a suitable cutter or glass, then place them on the baking sheet and dust with a little ground paprika. Bake 10 to 15 minutes or until well risen and golden brown. Cool briefly on a wire rack. Serve warm, if possible, with lots of butter.

PANTRY

Sunshine Lemon Pickles

Citrus fruits definitely add zest to the chilly winter months—pun intended! And lemons are far and away the favorite of most kitchen witches. Lemons are one of my five kitchen staples (the others being garlic, olive oil, fresh herbs, and feta cheese). They are sacred to the moon and carry her special powers of magic and divination, as well as protect us from the daily problems and stresses of life, giving hearts and minds a much-needed lift and boost.

This lemon pickle recipe was given to me by an Indian friend in South Africa. It is a wonderful spicy treat to have on hand in the winter pantry; not only can it be served as a side dish with curries and other spicy foods, but the pickles can be sprinkled over salads or just eaten as-is with cheese, cold meats, and bread.

Please note that the final quantity of pickle will depend on the size of your jars.

- 2 pounds thin-skinned lemons
- ½ cup sea salt
- 1 teaspoon turmeric
- 2 cups sugar
- 3 cups apple cider vinegar
- 2 teaspoons chili flakes
- 1 teaspoon garam masala (optional)
- ½ cup vegetable oil

Wash the lemons, then slice them thinly and remove the pips. (If they are large, cut the slices in half.) Place the slices in a large bowl, sprinkle with the salt, and leave to stand for a few hours.

In a medium saucepan, boil together the turmeric, sugar, vinegar, and spices until the sugar has dissolved and the mixture has thickened slightly. Remove from the heat and stir in the oil. Divide the lemon slices between suitable sterilized glass jars, shaking off any excess salt, then pour the cooled vinegar syrup over to cover them. Seal the jars and leave in a cool, dark place for at least two weeks before consuming; the pickles will keep well for a few months.

Honey, Herb, and Garlic Mustard

Spicy but not too strong, this mustard is an absolute pantry essential for the kitchen witch. It brightens up just about anything on a cold January day, from meat to cheese to hot dogs, fish, and salads. Mustard is such a powerful little spice, and it has been honored as such since time began, appearing frequently in Jewish, Christian, and Buddhist texts. It was sacred to Aesclepius, the Greek god of healing, and used to treat many ailments.

In the kitchen, quite apart from being a wonderful flavor enhancer, mustard is powerfully protective and also opens up our psychic abilities and third eye. Black mustard seeds protect us and help us access hidden realms of the spirit, while white mustard seeds are for faith, clarity, and prosperity.

> **4 tablespoons English mustard powder**
> **6 teaspoons black mustard seeds**
> **1 teaspoon each dried thyme and coriander**
> **1 teaspoon turmeric**
> **1 teaspoon salt**
> **1 tablespoon crushed garlic**
> **½ cup white wine vinegar**
> **½ cup white wine**
> **½ cup water**

2 tablespoons honey
1 tablespoon olive oil
½ cup light cream

In a small heavy-bottomed saucepan, combine the mustard powder, mustard seeds, thyme, coriander, turmeric, salt, and garlic. Mix to a paste with the vinegar and white wine. Add the water and slowly bring to a boil; stir in the honey and olive oil and continue cooking for 10 minutes, stirring often. The mixture should thicken up. Lastly, add the cream, stir well, and remove from the heat. You can process the mixture in a blender or food processor if you prefer a very smooth mustard. Once cool, spoon the mustard into small, sterilized pots or jars with tight-fitting lids. Keep in the refrigerator. The mustard lasts for at least 3 months.

Be there for others
but never leave
yourself behind...

Dodinsky

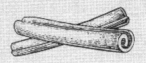

FEBRUARY

Sharing Love and Heart

With February comes the sacred feasts of Imbolc, Brigid, and Candlemas, all celebrated at the beginning of the month. In the ancient Celtic tradition, February 1 marked the first day of spring, even though it often doesn't feel much like spring yet, depending on where you live. Nevertheless, earth is slowly waking from her long winter slumber, and new growth and life are on the way. The days grow longer and brighter, and tiny green shoots start to emerge from the seemingly barren ground.

The feast of Candlemas symbolizes both hope and purification in the Celtic tradition. Marked by the lighting of

many candles, this feast reminds us of the gradual lighting of the world as the sun grows in strength, as well as the lighting of hope and new promise in our own hearts. And Brigid, the beautiful and fiery Irish goddess of poetry, creativity, healing, knowledge, and the flame, is the perfect symbol for our kitchens at this time. We might not have a cauldron, but we almost certainly have an oven, and that is our tool for creating magic in the heart of our homes and in our own hearts.

At Candlemas on February 2, honor Brigid by burning orange and gold candles and asking her blessing on your kitchens, not only at this time but all through the year. Ask her to guide you through this time of darkness toward the new light, the light of your fresh hopes and dreams for the coming year.

The Chinese New Year often takes place in early February and is marked by much feasting and celebrating as people honor the return of the kitchen (or stove) god, Zao Jhen or Zao Shen, after he has spent a few weeks with the Jade Emperor reporting on the behavior and good deeds/words of the people in his kitchen. (Apparently he was not above being bribed with a few sweet offerings, though!)

Valentine's Day is a more recent development in February, and to be honest it's a holiday I personally think is both overhyped and commercialized; for those who are

not in a romantic relationship of some kind, it can make us feel a little lonely or somehow inadequate. Nonetheless, the general principle of the day is a good one, and perhaps we can see it as being a larger "sharing of the heart" that embraces all around us, not just those who are (or could be) romantic partners. Love is who we are at our core, and our lives should always reflect this love that starts with ourselves and radiates outwards—and that is something we need to remember every day, not just on February 14.

As far as cooking is concerned, Imbolc is a celebration of things growing and flourishing anew (including young animals), so recipes with dairy products, eggs, grains, honey, and fish (for the watery sign of Pisces)—and, of course, chocolate—are all suitable for this month.

The Kitchen as a Sacred Space

For some of us, the kitchen is simply a utilitarian place, a necessary room for the storage, production, and consumption of food, although it is my hope that if you are reading this book, you also know that the kitchen can be so much more than that. It can truly be a sacred space, a place to gather and share, a creative place, a place of peace, healing, and meditation. All these things are possible in your kitchen; it just depends on your intention.

Creating a kitchen altar is one way of reflecting on this and honoring the kitchen and its place in our physical and spiritual lives. "Altar" does not always sit well with some people, though, accustomed as many of us are to thinking altars belong only in large and imposing places of worship and not in our homes. I tend to think of my kitchen altar as my "heart space"—a little part of my kitchen set aside for quiet reflection and memory.

And your own kitchen altar can be as simple as a little shelf, windowsill, or even a wooden tray, the only requirement being that it is safe from kitchen spills, fire, and the danger of being knocked over, especially if there are young children or pets around. What you put on your altar is also obviously very much a matter of personal preference and will also possibly change with the seasons. To reflect the bounty of a particular season as the year moves on, I keep a lovely old vase on mine and swap out flowers, herbs, leaves, and even a few beautiful feathers the birds have left for me.

I also like to place a simple cloth or covering on the altar and a single beautiful white or red candle in the middle. There are tiny framed photographs of a few special people whose memory I choose to honor in this way. Then there are the four earth elements, which can be symbolized in various ways:

WATER: a small bowl of pure spring water, a beautiful seashell

AIR: feathers or natural incense

FIRE: candles

EARTH: a tiny jar of sand or crystals (for more about crystals, see page 86)

I also keep a little jar or bowl of sea salt on the altar. When you come into the kitchen in the morning and again just before you leave at night, pause in front of your altar and pick up the bowl of salt. Scatter a few crystals in each of the four directions—north, south, east, and west—and say the following words quietly:

> *This is my magic place—a peaceful place.*
> *May all who come here be blessed and*
> *know that we are all connected to the earth*
> *and to each other. Here we are protected*
> *from all harmful forces and evil intent.*
> *Here we live our lives in joy, harmony, and*
> *love. May it ever be so—and so it is!*

Dinner for One

We will probably all have times during our lives when, through choice or circumstance, we cook and dine alone...and, if you are anything like me, although I am quite happy to spend an entire day planning and cooking a meal for others, it just doesn't seem worth it if I am on my own. Like so many people, it then becomes a case of scratching around to see what's in the fridge or eating a pot of yogurt or some leftover pizza while leaning on the kitchen counter reading the newspaper!

While obviously most of us wouldn't have the time or resources to prepare a three-course meal just for ourselves every day, I do believe that we need to treat ourselves with as much love and kindness as we would show to guests at our table; doing so honors and celebrates our own spirit and soul. The care we take of ourselves ripples out into the world and causes a growing circle of soul nurture, and it starts in our kitchens.

Is there a meal or dish you particularly enjoy but don't consider making if it's "just" you? Make it anyway! Set a place for yourself, light a candle, pour a glass of wine or sparkling water, and treat yourself as an honored and much-loved guest. Savor the moment—and the meal—with gratitude and love.

Do It Twice

If we have food to eat and a suitable, comfortable, and safe place in which to prepare it, we are already way ahead of the game in a world where so many have neither. I have a friend who truly loves to cook. She makes the most delicious soups in her slow cooker from various simple and inexpensive ingredients, and also all kinds of quick breads (the carrot and honey quick bread on page 54 is her recipe). Joan has a simple formula: whenever she makes something, she automatically doubles the recipe. One pot of soup or loaf of bread is for her family and she gives the other away, a sharing of her kitchen bounty that, as she says, doesn't cost her much financially but is infinitely rewarding in so many other ways.

I have started doing this myself—it's a lovely kitchen ritual, not only for this season but going forward through the year as well. Why not try it? You will find someone who truly welcomes your homemade offerings, I promise. Keep on doing it as often as is practically possible; above all, do it for yourself because your heart will just feel that much warmer on a chilly and gray day when the promise of spring still seems a long way off.

Kitchen Pleasures

- In so many cultures, pancakes are traditional in February, so why not have a pancake breakfast or brunch for family and friends? You can prepare a stack of your favorite pancakes and ask people to bring a selection of their favorite toppings or fillings. Have a pancake station where everyone can choose their own treats. It's a lot of fun on a chilly February day!

- To protect home and heart, burn a little cinnamon essential oil in a diffuser or melt a few drops on a white candle. Place the candle near your kitchen door or on a windowsill.

- On these days that can still be dark and cold, invoke warmth and light by using lots of citrus fruit with their healing and prosperous energies. Eat them raw, juice them, or cook with them— try making your own lemon marmalade or the lemon pickle recipe on page 34.

- Cooking is often equated with love, and rightly so, for it is an act that combines heart, body, and spirit. In February, consider to whom and how you can show love. Maybe we can create a special meal for someone we have fallen out with, and by this simple act we can extend the hand of loving friendship again.

- Create a spell jar for loving affection by placing dried rose petals, rosemary, lavender, and lemon balm in a small jar. Add a few rose quartz crystals and sprinkle with a little rose oil. Place the jar anywhere in your home where you need to create positive and loving vibes—and that includes the kitchen!

RECIPES

Creamy Fish Casserole with Herbed Crumble Topping

SERVES 4–6

Fish is linked with both Imbolc and Pisces, the astrological sign for February, so it makes the perfect meal at this time. I used to make it with a pastry topping, but these days I find this one lighter; the original recipe also only used whitefish, but I have added some shrimp for a little celebratory note—you can leave it out, though, if you prefer.

> 1½ cups water
>
> ½ cup dry white wine
>
> 1 small onion, chopped
>
> Salt and pepper to taste
>
> 1½ pounds firm whitefish fillets
>
> ½ pound small shrimp
>
> ¼ cup butter
>
> 2 tablespoons flour
>
> 1 cup heavy cream

2 tablespoons tomato puree

1 teaspoon Dijon mustard

2 tablespoons brandy (optional)

1 tablespoon chopped parsley

In a large saucepan, bring the water, wine, onion, salt, and pepper to boil. Cut the fillets in roughly 1½-inch chunks and add to the boiling water. Cook until just firm and opaque, then add the shrimp and cook for 5 minutes. Remove from the heat and keep the fish/shrimp covered in a bowl. Strain and reserve the cooking liquid.

In a deep pan, gently melt the butter, then stir in the flour to make a golden-brown paste. Add the reserved fish stock, stirring, until the mixture thickens. Stir in the cream, tomato, mustard, and brandy (if using). Stir the cooked fish and shrimp into this sauce and mix well; lastly, add the chopped parsley. Place the mixture into a well-greased casserole dish and preheat the oven to 350°F while you make the topping.

Crumble Topping

Place 1¼ cups all-purpose (plain) flour into a bowl, add ½ teaspoon salt, then rub in ½ cup chilled butter until the mixture looks like coarse breadcrumbs. Stir in 1 tablespoon finely snipped dill (or other herbs of your choice). Sprinkle the mixture evenly over the fish and then bake for 25 to 30

minutes or until the topping is browned and the fish mixture is sizzling. Serve hot.

Apple Pancakes with Honey Butter
MAKES ABOUT 1 DOZEN PANCAKES

There can't be a food culture in the world that doesn't have pancakes in it—whatever size, shape, or form they may take! They are universally popular and seem particularly appropriate as a heart-warming breakfast or brunch snack in the winter months.

It's amazing how the simple amalgamation of flour, egg, and milk, which form the basis of most pancake recipes, can be transmuted into something so delicious—but of course that is the essence of kitchen magic! And these pancakes have a little more magic, too, with the addition of apples, one of the most symbolic fruits since ancient times; they offer abundance, clarity, and protection, and are also known to help in love spells. Make these little pancakes for a magical winter morning breakfast that starts the day on a happily blessed note.

> 1½ cups all-purpose (plain) flour
> ¼ cup sugar
> 1 teaspoon baking powder
> ½ teaspoon salt
> 1 teaspoon ground cinnamon

2 eggs, separated
¼ cup oil or melted butter
¾ cup apple puree
½ cup buttermilk
Oil for frying

Sift the first five dry ingredients together in a large bowl and set aside. In another bowl, beat together the egg yolks, oil or butter, apple puree, and buttermilk until they form a smooth batter. Pour into the flour mixture and mix well. Beat the egg whites in a grease-free glass bowl until they are stiff but not dry, then fold them into the batter mixture.

Heat a little oil in a skillet and fry the pancakes, using about ¼ cup batter for each pancake and only frying two or three at a time. When bubbles appear on the surface of each pancake, flip it over and fry till light golden brown. Keep the cooked pancakes warm while you cook the others and serve topped with lots of honey butter.

Honey Butter

Place ½ cup unsalted and softened butter in a bowl, and gradually beat in ½ cup raw or organic honey. It should be fairly runny, otherwise it won't blend well with the butter. Lastly, you can stir in any of these optional ingredients: ½ teaspoon ground cinnamon or nutmeg or 1 tablespoon of finely grated lemon or orange rind.

Creamy Rice Pudding

SERVES 6

Rice is, of course, not only a staple food for a very large percentage of the world's population, but it's also imbued with many magical properties—chiefly, it's seen as a symbol of abundance, rich blessings, and also of fertility. In this meaning fertility can be seen in the larger sense—of the fruitfulness and possibility we all carry within ourselves that hopefully will see the birth of new and wonderful things in this new year.

Rice pudding is also such a comforting, nurturing dish, perfect for cold nights. If you prefer a slightly less rich version, you can make it with all milk, omitting the cream. I personally love to make this dish with either basmati or jasmine rice: not only does it cook to a beautiful softness, but these rice varieties also have a subtle fragrance of their own.

Preheat the oven to 350°F. Butter a medium oval or rectangular baking dish well.

> **4 eggs, separated**
> **½ cup sugar**
> **1 teaspoon vanilla or almond extract**
> **1 cup milk**
> **1 cup cream**
> **2 tablespoons all-purpose (plain) flour**

1 teaspoon baking powder

½ teaspoon salt

2 cups cooked, cooled rice

2 tablespoons butter, melted

Ground cinnamon

Strawberry or raspberry preserves

In a large bowl, beat egg yolks, sugar and extract together very well. Stir in the milk and cream, then add the flour, baking powder, and salt, and mix well until smooth. Add the rice and melted butter. Beat the egg whites in a grease-free glass bowl until they are stiff but not dry, then fold gently into the rice mixture. Pour into the baking dish and sprinkle with a little ground cinnamon.

Bake 40 to 50 minutes or until the pudding is set, risen, and golden brown on top. Serve warm topped with a spoonful of fruit preserves or simply with more cream! It also tastes good cold.

Carrot and Honey Quick Bread

MAKES 1 MEDIUM LOAF OR 12 MUFFINS

This simple quick bread is not too sweet, and it also makes delicious muffins; above all, its warm golden color and flavor makes it the perfect celebration for Brigid's Day, the bright and beautiful Celtic goddess. Serve it with soups and casseroles or just sliced with lots of butter and some creamy cheese. The humble carrot is endowed with many magical properties, too: fertility, passion, and the dawning of new light and clarity. Add some chopped sunflower seeds to this recipe for even more spring magic.

Preheat oven to 350°F.

Butter a medium loaf or bread pan well.

> 1 cup all-purpose (plain) flour
>
> 1 cup whole wheat flour
>
> 3 teaspoons baking powder
>
> 1 teaspoon ground cinnamon or nutmeg
>
> ½ teaspoon salt
>
> 2 large carrots, peeled and finely grated
>
> 1 egg
>
> ½ cup vegetable oil
>
> 2 tablespoons brown sugar
>
> ¾ cup buttermilk (or milk)
>
> ½ cup honey
>
> ½ cup golden raisins (optional)

In a large bowl, sift together the flours, baking powder, spices, and salt. Stir in the finely grated carrots. In a separate bowl, beat the egg, oil, brown sugar, buttermilk, and honey together. Make a well in the center of the dry ingredients, add the liquid, and stir quickly until just combined and forming a batter—don't overbeat. Lastly, mix in the raisins (if using) and then spoon the batter into the prepared pan.

Bake 23 to 30 minutes or until the bread is risen and golden brown. Turn out onto a wire rack to cool. This bread is best eaten within a day or two of baking.

Hot Chocolate with a Kick

MAKES 2 SERVINGS

Those of us who have read Joanne Harris's *Chocolat* or seen the movie will remember how the mysterious heroine, Vianne, brought her magic (and chocolate creations) to the little village of Lansquenet-sous-Tannes and everybody's lives were changed in enchanted ways. She had a particular way with hot chocolate, too—one I have tried to emulate here. The base of this recipe is actually a delicious chocolate sauce that can be kept in the fridge and also used to pour over ice cream, cake, or simply to spoon furtively out of the jar when noone else is around. Share this hot chocolate with someone you love on a frosty February night.

1½ cups sugar

½ cup light golden syrup, honey, or maple syrup

¾ cup cocoa powder

½ cup water

1 teaspoon vanilla extract

½ teaspoon salt

2 cups whole milk

3 tablespoons chocolate sauce

½ teaspoon ground chili (optional)

2 tablespoons brandy (optional)

To make the chocolate sauce, mix the first six ingredients in a medium saucepan and cook over low heat, stirring continuously, until they are combined and the sauce is dark and glossy. Allow to cool before pouring into a sterilized glass jar. Keep in the fridge.

To make two delicious cups of hot chocolate, pour the whole milk into a saucepan and gradually add the chocolate sauce and chili (if using); bring to a simmer, stirring well, until the chocolate sauce has melted into the milk. Stir in the brandy, then pour into two warmed cups or glasses and serve right away. To warm cups, place them in warm (not hot), clean water for 10 to 15 minutes, dry, and fill with drinks.

PANTRY

Making Your Own Butter

There is something highly satisfying and magical about the process of making butter, even if it is probably not something one would do every day. I also like the fact that it allows one to control the amount of salt added—or, indeed, flavor the butter in other creative ways.

To make about ½ pound butter, you will need 2 cups heavy cream at room temperature. Pour the cream into a large glass or stainless bowl. Using a hand mixer, start whipping it, gradually at first and then increasing the speed. The cream will initially thicken and then start to separate out, forming a thick mass surrounded by liquid (this is the whey, or buttermilk).

Pour off the liquid (keep it for baking or bread making) and place the lump of butter in a bowl of cold water, to rinse any remaining buttermilk away. Using your hands, gradually work ½ teaspoon salt or other flavoring into the

butter and form into a log or roll. Wrap in plastic wrap (cling film) and keep refrigerated. Other possible flavorings include freshly ground black pepper, dried herbs, or a little fresh crushed garlic. Use the butter within a week.

Chinese Stir-Fry Sauce
MAKES ABOUT 1½ CUPS

I like to keep a bottle of this sauce in my pantry at all times. Unlike some commercial versions, it contains no preservatives or MSG and is really simple to make. Use it when making a chicken, vegetable, or fish stir-fry, or add a few teaspoons to rice or noodle dishes. It contains lots of bright, uplifting flavors like ginger, chili, and coriander. The sauce will keep well for a month or so in a cool, dry place—just remember to shake it well before using.

> 2 tablespoons honey or molasses
> ½ cup rice vinegar
> 4 tablespoons soy (soya) sauce
> 2 tablespoons lime (or lemon) juice
> 1 green chili, thinly sliced
> 1 teaspoon crushed garlic
> 1 teaspoon finely chopped ginger
> 1 teaspoon ground coriander
> ½ cup sesame oil

Mix all the ingredients except the oil together in a bowl; pour the mixture into a suitable bottle. Pour in the oil and shake well before putting the lid on the bottle. Use as suggested above, shaking the mixture well each time.

That is one good thing about this world ... there are always sure to be more springs.

L M Montgomery

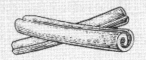

MARCH

Flowering and Fresh

The spring equinox occurs around March 20–23 in the northern hemisphere and marks the transition from the cold months of winter to the bright green promise of spring, even if the temperature outside is still on the chilly side! Ostara—or Oestre or Eostre, as it was known in ancient days—is a season of new energies, fertility, and manifestation. The name actually comes from Germany, as Eostre was the German goddess of fertility; it was later taken over by the Christian holiday of Easter, with the same obvious themes of resurrection, rebirth, and new life. This particular holiday sometimes seems to be a little lost nowadays, but it remains a very special time for planning new joys and directions, using the seeds we planted (spiritually and emotionally) at the time of Imbolc. The year is moving to new warmth and growth, and hopefully so are we; in our kitchens, too, we can create and share the fresh alchemy of spring.

The Faery Goddess of Herbs and Healing

Airmid (pronounced *are-mith*) is not generally seen as a kitchen goddess, but I have chosen to include her here because she is the faery goddess linked to herbs, healing, and green power, and that is something of vital importance to us in both our kitchens and our lives.

Airmid was one of the Tuatha de Danann, the Shining Ones, of Ireland. Beautiful and gentle, she is a healer who came by her knowledge of all plants and herbs after the tragic murder of her brother. She is the keeper of herbal magic and wisdom and can guide us to the plants best suited in helping us on both physical and spiritual levels. In much the same way as the garden, the kitchen is a place of magic and enchantment where we can create healing, joy, and peace for ourselves and others.

I love Airmid and often invoke her gentle wisdom, particularly when I am working with herbs and other plants in the kitchen. This ritual is a simple way of inviting her

presence and help at any time. Light a beautiful green candle and gather a bunch of fresh green herbs or other wild green offerings. Place the herbs in a small jug or glass next to the candle and add a small bowl of salt sprinkled with your favorite floral or herbal essential oils; I particularly like using mint, basil, lavender, or lemon oils.

Light the candle. The best time to do this is either in the early morning or in the soft light of late afternoon.

Softly say the following, gazing at the light:

> *Beautiful Airmid, keeper of herbs and*
> *all green plant magic, guide me to the*
> *wonders that you know. Teach me the gifts*
> *of healing and joy hidden in these green*
> *messengers. Let the natural wonders heal*
> *me and my world, and bring us all back to*
> *a place of true and vital joy and restoration*
> *in body, mind, and spirit. And so it is.*

Eggs: Symbols of the Season

Simple, humble, and often taken a little for granted in our kitchens, eggs are a traditional symbol of spring and its many blessings. Their shells hold perfect new growth and possibility, not unlike the child cradled in the womb.

My very creative mother used to teach children's arts and crafts classes when I was young, and in spring she

always had an egg decorating class where the children could paint the blown chicken eggs she gave them or decorate them in other ways—glitter, paper cutouts, and more. I also made some over the years and recently, tidying out my mother's things after her passing, was touched to discover a small box of my little egg creations, wrapped in tissue paper and stored by her all these years. Now, in spring, these little eggs will be displayed in a basket on my kitchen shelf, a reminder of the new life, hope, and spirit we can discover in this magical season, the "cracking open" of our shells to discover our true and beautiful selves.

A lovely kitchen ritual would be to gather a few family and friends to spend an afternoon making and decorating their own eggs in a way that reflects their personal hopes and intentions for the new season. Tea and cake (made from the contents of the blown eggs) are a nice accompaniment after each person has shared the wishes and hopes shown in their egg creation. Afterwards, separately or as a group, say the following:

> *Earth energy is changing. It is growing*
> *new seeds, new possibilities, and natural*
> *magic—beautiful changes. I, too, am*
> *changing like the seasons. There are choices*
> *and changes for growth and hope. What*
> *seeds do I need to plant and incubate like the*

embryo in the egg? I ask the goddess, spirits,
and earth energies to guide me in my new
direction. With grace and hope it is born and
nurtured, and it will grow. And so it is.

Living This Moment

As spring moves in and the sun comes up earlier, it's a good time to start rising a little earlier and enjoying the first light of the day. This is a very special time, and according to folk lore and mythology, it is also the time we are at our most creative and most open to accessing the spirit realm. For this reason, I would encourage us all to spend a little time sitting quietly in the kitchen in the very early morning—with open windows, if the weather is warm enough, so you can also be saluted by the dawn chorus of the birds.

Make a cup of tea or coffee, find a comfortable spot, and simply be in the moment for a while—this is really the way to find the true enchantment in the everyday. Only by being fully present in the here and now, even if we are doing something as simple as sipping some aromatic drink, can we truly find the mindful moment; time seems to become less important, and we start to feel the depth that lies beneath even the smallest action. In this moment of focus things become clearer, and we can truly appreciate what we have, who we are ... and the magic of it all.

This is mindfulness: a moment when we focus on a single thought or idea—just one thing. Everything else can wait. And the kitchen is the perfect place to start doing this with tasks that demand and need our undivided attention. Slicing the tomatoes and smelling their sun-ripened goodness, crushing the pungent garlic cloves, whipping a bowl of cream and watching it turn into white, fluffy clouds ... this is the stuff of magic.

Whatever we are doing, we need to just enjoy it, there and then; later we can think and worry about the next moment or hour or day. Mindfulness feeds us, and I don't mean literally; it reminds us of the magic in ourselves and in the everyday details of our lives, and the kitchen is a good place to start that journey of discovery.

Eat Your Greens!

Perhaps, like me, you grew up being told to eat your vegetables—and hating it! I tried all sorts of sneaky ways to hide them on my plate (especially peas, beans, and broccoli), but somehow my mother always caught on. Only years later did I truly come to appreciate the wonder of vegetables: yet another example of the beautiful gifts of our earth, they also carry her fertile, grounding energy and have lots of magical associations, too.

Try to eat vegetables in season whenever possible, for that is when they hold their best and most effective energy. If you can't grow your own, buy them fresh and preferably organically grown (the farmer's market is a great place for this).

Some magical associations for common vegetables:

BEANS: family ties and love, wisdom, abundance

BROCCOLI: abundance and strength

CARROTS: health, fertility, clarity of thought, passion

CAULIFLOWER: working with moon energy, emotional healing, protection

CELERY: love, clarity, focus

CUCUMBER: peace and calm; also good for healing after illness

LEEKS: protection, love magic, purification

LETTUCE: peace, harmony, meditative calm

MUSHROOMS: potent moon magic and also strength, bravery, and healing

ONION: physical and spiritual protection, prosperity

PEAS: love and abundance, sacred to the hearth goddesses

POTATOES: emotional grounding, protection, and abundance

PUMPKIN & SQUASH: harmony, abundance, working with the spirit world

SPINACH: passion, fertility, and strength

TOMATO: love, passion, protection, and generally bringing a positive vibe to your kitchen (although they are technically a fruit, I've chosen to include them here)

Now there's no reason not to eat your greens and find interesting new ways of preparing them over the seasons of the year.

Kitchen Pleasures

- On March 16, the Spicy Fire Festival in India, why not make a wonderfully aromatic curry or other spicy dish? The warmth of these dishes gives us a delicious reminder that soon summer will be here again.

- Keep a few bunches of parsley in your kitchen or on your altar as an offering to Persephone, goddess of the underworld. She helps us connect with those who have left us on the physical plane and are now in spirit.

- Spring is the season of air and of words, creativity, and communication, so why not write some of your favorite words, quotes, or affirmations on small pieces of paper and pin them up in your kitchen or add them to your altar? Create a small jar or bowl dedicated to these words of wisdom and pull one out each morning to reflect on quietly before the day begins.

- On International Women's Day, March 8, honor yourself and all the woman who have influenced you on any level and in any way by spending time with the women who are important in your life: mothers, sisters, daughters, friends. Have tea and something good to eat, sit at your kitchen table, and remember that women truly rock this world!

- Prepare a simple broth using the fresh young vegetables of spring—peas, asparagus, chives, baby potatoes, nettles, and wild garlic (if you are lucky enough to find it). Savor the broth, feeling the bright light of spring filling you up on every level.

- Make a cardamom and orange tea for those days when spring seems to be a long way off. Place 3–4 lightly crushed cardamom seeds in a jug and pour 1 cup boiling water over them. Add the rind of ½ a small orange, 2 teaspoons of chamomile tea, and a sprig of mint, if you have it. Steep for 10 minutes, then strain and serve warm.

Spring Blessing Quiche

SERVES 6–8 AS A LIGHT MEAL

This is a wonderful way to use up the eggs left after blowing eggs for decorating and ceremony.

This quiche is crustless, making it both lighter and easy to prepare. It can be served warm or even chilled (which is how I actually prefer it) for brunch or a light lunch, with a few salad leaves on the side, in keeping with the green and springlike theme. For fairly obvious reasons, asparagus is a symbol of sexuality and life force, merging with the fertility of the eggs. You can use fresh asparagus spears, steamed lightly for 5 to 10 minutes, or canned asparagus, well drained, will also work.

Preheat oven to 350°F. Grease a deep 9- or 10-inch pie plate very well.

2 tablespoons each butter and olive oil

4 ounces small white mushrooms, sliced

A few scallions, thinly sliced

6 eggs

1 cup milk or light cream, divided

¼ cup flour

1 teaspoon baking powder

Salt and pepper to taste

¾ cup grated Cheddar cheese

10–12 asparagus spears

2 tablespoons chopped chives

¼ cup grated Parmesan

Heat the butter and olive oil in a saucepan and fry the mushrooms and scallions gently for a few minutes, until soft but not brown. Remove from the heat, pat dry with paper towels (kitchen paper) to remove excess oil, and cool.

In a large bowl, beat the eggs very well, until they are soft and light yellow in color. In a cup, mix 2 tablespoons of the milk or cream with the flour, baking powder, salt, and pepper to make a smooth paste, then stir this into the egg mixture, together with the rest of the milk or cream, and beat again very well. Stir the mushrooms, scallions, and Cheddar into the mixture, then pour it into the prepared pie plate. Carefully arrange the asparagus spears around the top of the mixture in a circle, with the tips of the asparagus

facing outward, like the rays of the sun. Sprinkle the chives and Parmesan over the surface of the quiche and bake it in the preheated oven for 25 to 30 minutes or until the filling is set, a little puffed up, and pale golden brown. Serve from the dish either warm or cold.

Spiced Fish

SERVES AT LEAST 6

This is based on a Cape Malay recipe from South Africa, where it is a very popular traditional meal for springtime and Easter celebrations, generally served with salad and lots of fresh bread to mop up the tasty sauce. Fish is, of course, associated with the element of water and as such carries the energies of cleansing, purification, fertility, and abundance. This is a recipe easily adapted as regards quantities of spice—and best of all, it keeps well in the fridge for a week or more.

> 2 pounds firm whitefish fillets, skinless
> ¾ cup all-purpose (plain) flour
> Salt and pepper to taste
> 2 eggs, beaten
> Vegetable oil
> 1 cup apple cider vinegar
> 1 cup water
> ½ cup brown sugar

2 onions, sliced thinly

3 garlic cloves, crushed

1 tablespoon curry powder

½ teaspoon turmeric

½ teaspoon chili powder

½ teaspoon ground cumin

Cut the fish into large cubes. Season flour with salt and pepper, then dip the pieces of fish in the beaten eggs before coating with the flour mixture. Shallow fry the fish in batches until golden brown and cooked through. Drain on paper towels (kitchen paper), cool, and place the fish pieces in a large nonmetallic dish, preferably glass.

In a large saucepan, simmer the remaining ingredients until the onion and garlic are soft and transparent and the spices are dissolved in the sauce. Cool for a few minutes, then pour the warm sauce over the fish. Cover the dish and keep it in the refrigerator for at least 2–3 hours before serving to ensure the flavors are infused. If you like, serve sprinkled with fresh cilantro or lemon leaves.

Crispy Potato Fritters

MAKES ABOUT 10–12

And another Irish favorite: potatoes! Actually, these little fritters are just about everyone's favorite, and they bring with them the grounding and peaceful energy of potatoes. This recipe can easily be doubled—trust me, it's often

necessary! The fritters make a delicious snack or can be used as a side dish with just about any main course.

- **2–3 medium potatoes, peeled**
- **2 tablespoons grated onion (optional)**
- **3 tablespoons flour**
- **1 teaspoon baking powder**
- **1 egg, beaten**
- **Salt and pepper to taste**
- **Chopped chives/parsley to taste**
- **Vegetable oil for frying**

Grate the potatoes coarsely. Place in a large bowl and mix in the grated onion (if using), flour, and baking powder. Stir in the egg, salt, pepper, and herbs and mix to form a sticky batter. Heat a little oil in a heavy-bottomed frying pan, and place tablespoonfuls of the mixture into the pan—only fry 4 or 5 at a time. Fry for 10 to 15 minutes, turning frequently, until the fritters are golden brown and fully cooked. Drain well on paper towels (kitchen paper) and serve warm with the sour cream dipping sauce.

Sour Cream Dipping Sauce

Combine 1 cup sour cream with 2 teaspoons fresh lemon juice, 3 tablespoons snipped fresh chives (or other herb of your choice), 1 small clove of garlic, crushed, and a little freshly ground black pepper. Mix well and chill until serving time.

Irish Coffee Brownies

MAKES 9–12 LARGE BROWNIES

Still on the Irish theme … this is something that would be gobbled up by the little men in green—or just about anyone else, I would imagine. This is my basic brownie recipe but given an extra boost of clarity and energy by the addition of coffee, which is definitely my favorite beverage (what can I say, I'm half Italian). The whiskey ties into the Irish coffee theme too; when I am serving these for dessert, I also top each brownie with a fat swirl of whipped cream and a dusting of espresso powder. The luck of the Irish to you!

Preheat oven to 325°F. Grease a 9-inch square baking pan very well or line with parchment (baking) paper.

> 1½ sticks butter
>
> 1½ cups brown sugar
>
> ¾ cup unsweetened cocoa
>
> ¼ cup strong coffee
>
> 3 eggs
>
> ¾ cup flour
>
> ½ teaspoon salt
>
> 2 tablespoons Irish whiskey
>
> ½ cup chocolate chips (optional)

In a large saucepan, gently melt together the butter and brown sugar, then stir in the cocoa and coffee to make a thick mixture. Remove from the heat and cool for about 5

minutes, then beat in the eggs one at a time. Sift the flour and salt together, then add to the butter mixture, beating well to make a smooth batter. Stir in the whiskey and the chocolate chips (if using). Spread the batter evenly in the pan and bake 30 to 35 minutes, until the brownies are a little crisp on top; to test they are done, insert a thin skewer into the mixture—if it comes out with just a few moist crumbs attached, they are ready. Don't overbake—brownies should have a squidgy texture.

Cool the brownies in the pan, then cut into squares using a long-bladed knife. Remove carefully from the pan and store in an airtight tin or container. They last for a few days, but that has never happened in my experience.

Cheese Wafers
MAKES ABOUT 40 WAFERS

One of the nicest things about making cookies, either sweet or savory, as here, is that one can use them to create all sorts of magical intentions simply by adding herbs, spices, and other ingredients to the basic cookie. I love these cheese wafers—they were one of the first things I ever baked—but these days I enjoy adding extra taste dimensions to give them a little enchanted edge. For these cheese cookies, I have chosen to add chili (in the form of cayenne pepper) for its creative and passionate energies, and also a tiny hint

of mustard, which helps us see more clearly on every level and access our psychic powers.

Preheat oven to 350°F. Grease a large baking sheet well or line it with parchment (baking) paper.

1 stick unsalted butter, softened
1 cup finely shredded Cheddar cheese
1½ cups flour
½ teaspoon cayenne pepper
½ teaspoon salt
¼ teaspoon dry mustard powder

In a large bowl, cream the butter and cheese together very well to form a soft and fluffy mixture. Gradually add the flour and flavorings, mixing to form a fairly soft dough. If the dough is too soft to handle, you can place it in the refrigerator for 30 minutes.

Roll the dough into small balls (about ¾ inch in diameter) and arrange on the baking sheet, leaving space between each. Using the base of a glass, press each ball down firmly until it is fairly thin—about ⅛ inch. Bake the wafers for about 10 minutes or until pale golden (you may have to bake a few batches, depending on the size of your oven). Allow to cool and crisp up for a few moments before carefully lifting the wafers onto a wire rack. They are fragile so should be stored in airtight containers in layers. They last for a week or more but are usually gobbled up quickly since they are quite addictive.

PANTRY

Leprechaun Pesto

MAKES ABOUT ¾ CUP

This deliciously green pesto is dedicated to the little green Irish sprites known as leprechauns. Although mischievous by nature, they are also known to be helpful around the house if they are treated with respect and kindness—and since they keep their pots of gold safely stored at the end of the rainbow, it's always wise to keep in their good books. This pesto simply sings of spring with its fresh green flavors and is wonderful served with potatoes and other vegetables or over grilled fish or chicken. A spoonful can also be added to sauces, dips, and salad dressings or drizzled over pizza and flatbreads.

Chives have been used since medieval times and are renowned for removing negative and destructive energies while imparting protection for the home. I like to use parsley with the chives, as it seems to balance their onion flavor; of course, parsley is also a powerful herb in its own

right with both uplifting and purifying qualities. It's also supposed to help in communing with the spirit world—and was apparently used by good witches to help them fly! If you want to make the pesto more traditional, add ½ cup finely chopped pecans, walnuts, or almonds when processing the mixture.

> **1 cup fresh chives**
> **1 cup fresh flatleaf parsley**
> **1 clove garlic, crushed**
> **½ cup olive oil**
> **2 tablespoons Parmesan cheese (optional)**
> **Salt and pepper to taste**

Combine all the ingredients in a food processor or blender, and blend until fairly smooth. You may need to add a little extra olive oil or lemon juice if the mixture seems dry. Store in a glass jar in the refrigerator, where it will keep for several weeks.

Rhubarb and Rosemary Preserve

MAKES THREE OR FOUR 4-OUNCE JARS

Rhubarb is a bright harbinger of spring bounty, and it's also a protective and magical fruit that apparently was used during the Great Plague of medieval times to keep one from harm or death … hopefully with some success. Beautiful and beloved rosemary is, of course, also a herb linked with healing, protection, and encouraging happy and peaceful memories. I love serving this simple preserve with scones and breads, and it also goes particularly well with cheese.

> **1½ pounds fresh or frozen rhubarb, chopped**
> **1½ cups sugar**
> **Juice and zest of 1 large lemon**
> **¼ cup honey**
> **A few finely chopped rosemary sprigs**
> **Pinch of cinnamon**

Place the rhubarb, sugar, lemon juice and zest, and honey in a large heavy-bottomed saucepan and simmer very gently until the sugar has dissolved completely and the mixture is thick. Remove from the heat and stir in the rosemary and cinnamon. Cool completely before spooning into small sterilized jars, and keep in the fridge once open.

*R*ight now you have
everything you need
to be in bliss ...

Anthony de Mello

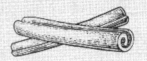

APRIL

Festivals and Bright Energy

April leads us into the later part of spring, although it is still bright with the energy of new growth and hope. In spring we also grow as we germinate new ideas, dreams, and ways of being. This month is a good one to look at the foods we choose and prepare on a daily basis, and to perhaps make some changes to our meals in order to best support both increased metabolism and energy, which we need at this time.

Fresh green foods are starting to be abundant and should form part of our kitchen choices; they are rich in minerals and fiber, helpful to bodies that might still be a bit sluggish from the winter. Above all, we need to remember that we are energy, just like the earth herself, and like the earth our energies are changing and shifting.

Keep your kitchen warm and bright—remember, April is often also the season of chilly winds and rain showers! Place a few pots of bright daffodils or narcissus on your kitchen table, and invite the flower fae to come and visit. They are always happy to share their magic energies as long as you treat them with kindness and respect (and maybe leave a few small cakes or a dish of honey out for them in the kitchen at night when everyone has gone to bed).

Kitchen Journal Dreams

Your kitchen journal is the perfect place to dream—starting with food, of course! What foods would you like to taste, experience, or learn how to make in this spring season? Where would you like to travel to have these festive meals? For example, I love Greek food but have never been to Greece; however, I dream of enjoying a traditional Greek meal one day, complete with ouzo, sitting on a terrace overlooking that amazingly dark blue sea…a really *Mamma Mia* scene!

Maybe going to a particular place or country isn't on your agenda right now, but what could you do to create that magic right in your own kitchen? That's the beauty of

food and recipes: they can be a magic carpet ride to a different world of taste and flavor.

And, following on from this, what else do you hope to grow in your life this spring season? Maybe it's travel and a change of scenery or maybe it's something a little deeper, like simplifying your lifestyle or moving on from a situation or relationship that you have outgrown. Be honest, and let spring magic open you up to new thoughts and possibilities.

Saying Grace ... Being Grace

Perhaps, like me, you grew up with the tradition of joining hands and saying grace before mealtimes—and perhaps, also like so many of us, you no longer do. Food, like so many other good things, has become a victim of our busyness; we eat in a rush, sometimes on the run, and no longer take the time to gather quietly together around the table and simply be present, for the food and for each other. That is the essence of grace ... being present and grateful for all those who have helped bring this food to us—be it the plants and animals, the farmers and storekeepers and those who cook and serve it. Whatever our spiritual path, grace offers us a moment to open up to the true blessing that is our lives and honor and celebrate the magic that brings us food to nourish bodies, minds, and souls.

Another simple way to honor our food and our lives is to say a simple grace anytime we start working in our kitchen, gathering ingredients, or preparing a meal.

I am grateful, here, in this moment. Here is
this food, here is this abundance and grace
for me and all those who will share this meal.
I am grateful. I am blessed. And so it is.

Crystals for Your Kitchen

Stones and crystals are an intrinsic, ancient, and magical part of our earth; beautiful and uplifting, they are sacred gifts from nature and can be used in many wonderful ways in our homes and lives to create natural healing and magical energy—and our kitchens are no exception.

I have chosen a few of my favorite crystals and stones here. They are generally fairly easy to obtain and can be used in different ways for kitchen magic. I like to keep a few crystals on my kitchen altar and add them to kitchen spell bottles and wish jars; they can also be tucked into little fabric pouches with herbs and other offerings to make magic bags. Crystal essences work in a similar way to flower essences and can be used in ceremonies of protection or purification, or simply sprinkled around the corners of your kitchen or added to kitchen sprays.

To make crystal essences, simply take a glass bowl of spring water and place a few of your chosen crystals in the water. Ensure that your crystals are suitable for immersion in liquid, as some, like selenite, are not. Leave the bowl outside under the full moon for a night, after which time the water will have absorbed the magical and therapeutic essences of the crystals. Remove the crystals and dry them; carefully pour the water into smaller dark glass bottles and keep in a cool place. (For this idea, I am indebted to Tess Whitehurst and her lovely book *Magical Housekeeping*.)

AMETHYST: this is probably my favorite crystal. Delicate and beautiful, it's a powerful healing stone for body and mind, and it supports us in finding abundance, peace, and calm.

AQUAMARINE: a stone imbued with sea energies and purifying qualities, it clears and calms the atmosphere after emotional or psychic storms of any kind.

CITRINE: a light, sunny, and happy crystal, one that brings healing energies, renewed creativity, and abundance on every level.

CLEAR QUARTZ: a wonderful all-purpose crystal that increases good energies and brings about a healing and peaceful vibration wherever it is used.

HEMATITE: an ancient stone, the mineral form of iron oxide, which comes in a number of differing colors, from soft red to metallic gray. It's a strongly protective stone and should be used to protect boundaries on every level: personal, spiritual, or within the home in general.

JADE: green and translucent, jade makes us think of nature in all her beauty. It's been honored and used in China for thousands of years as a symbol of purity, abundance, and spiritual power. Jade should be used whenever we want to elevate feelings of well-being on a personal or practical plane.

MOONSTONE: a beautiful lunar stone, sharing the moon's sacred energies and magic; I love using this stone when I need greater intuition or creativity.

ROSE QUARTZ: keep this pretty and sparkling crystal close when you want to feel more loving or bring more love into your life; more than that, though, it will help us open our hearts to all the aspects of our lives and embrace ourselves just as we are.

Happy, Healthy Kitchen

Without being obsessive about it, the simple truth is that kitchens do get dirty and food preparation sometimes makes a mess! Kitchens need to be cleaned, not only to keep them healthy and fresh, but also as a way of ensuring their energy remains clean and bright, an energy which then passes into us and the work we do in our kitchens.

Obviously it's possible to buy an array of kitchen cleaning and hygiene products, many of which are also environmentally friendly, but I prefer to use the ingredients I have right at my disposal in my pantry or refrigerator to make my own simple and effective products, which also usually represent quite a saving in cost.

These are just a few simple ideas to try in your own kitchen:

A Basic Cleaner for Kitchen Surfaces

Combine 1 teaspoon salt, 1 tablespoon baking soda, a few drops either lemon or lemongrass essential oil and a cup of spring water. Place in a spray bottle and use to mop up spills, grease, and the like.

Rosemary and Lavender Air Freshener

Combine ½ cup each spirit vinegar and spring water in a spray bottle. Add ¼ cup vodka and 5 drops each rosemary and lavender essential oils. Shake well before use. This will

89

keep for a few weeks in a cool, dry place. You can also add a few fresh rosemary sprigs to the bottle, but they will soften and go a bit brown with time!

Washing-Up Liquid

You will need unscented castile soap (such as Dr. Bronner's) for this recipe. Mix ½ cup grated soap with 1 teaspoon borax, 1 tablespoon baking soda, and 5 drops each lemon and lavender essential oil. Pour 1½ cups hot spring water over the mixture and stir until dissolved, stirring frequently to make a smooth mixture. Cool, pour into a clean soap dispenser, and use to wash dishes, as well as for general kitchen cleanup.

Kitchen Pleasures

- On April 1, April Fool's Day, enjoy having fun with food. Have dessert for breakfast or serve a meal in the opposite order. Eat things that you really loved to eat as a child—as messily as possible, with your hands. Remember life—and food—don't always have to be a serious matter, so be light in spirit today. One of my favorite things when I was young was Rice Krispie treats, those sticky ones made with marshmallows: in honor of the child within, I always make a pan of those at the beginning of April!

- After the first spring rains, gather a little of the water in a beautiful small glass bottle or jar. Place it on your altar and give thanks for the life-giving rain that sustains our earth and brings us such abundance. Later you can use the water to sprinkle over your kitchen herbs or simply dip your fingers in it before starting to cook.

- On a spring morning, wake up your body and spirit with this infusion: combine a little sliced ginger root, lemon zest and juice, a slice of apple, and a little honey in a jug, then top up with boiling water and stir. Strain and drink while it's warm.

- Decorate your kitchen with lots of spring colors: green apples, sprays of blossom or willow, and candles of pale rose, mauve, and gold.

- If you only ever make fried or scrambled eggs, try something different: eggs baked in cream (*en cocotte*) or shakshuka, a spicy onion and tomato sauce with fried eggs on top. Mop up everything with lots of bread!

RECIPES

Salsa Salad

SERVES 4

This spring salad is so full of sparkling and fresh flavors it makes a wonderful dish by itself. Served with a bowl of warmed tortilla chips topped with grated cheese to continue the Mexican theme, it's an energizing dish for a warm and bright April day! Mangoes, by the way, are sacred to the Buddha and have been credited with inciting feelings of love and passion—and, perhaps not incidentally, with fertility, too.

> 1 cup baby lettuce/cabbage, shredded
> 1 large avocado, peeled and diced
> 1 mango, peeled and cut into cubes
> 1 cup baby tomatoes, halved
> 1 red onion, sliced
> 1 yellow or red pepper, cut into small dice
> A handful of fresh radishes (optional)
> A handful of fresh cilantro (coriander) leaves, chopped

½ cup olive or vegetable oil

¼ cup fresh lime or lemon juice

1 clove garlic, crushed

1 red chili, chopped fine

¼ teaspoon ground cumin

Fresh mint leaves, chopped, for garnish

Combine the ingredients up to and including the fresh cilantro (coriander) in a large salad bowl. In a small bowl or jug, combine the remaining ingredients (excluding the mint leaves) and mix well to make a dressing. Pour over the salad and mix lightly but well. Top with the chopped mint leaves and serve.

Lamb and Mint Soup

SERVES 8–10

This gentle and satisfying soup is both delicious and filled with healing and spiritual properties. Lamb can be fairly expensive, but with this recipe you can feed quite a crowd. The recipe is traditional to both Greece and Turkey, with some variations, and is often served around Easter or at wedding celebrations. Lamb is, of course, a symbol of new life and fertility, and mint has both protective and calming energies. The original recipe for this soup also includes egg yolks, but I have chosen to omit them to make the soup lighter in taste and easier to prepare.

1 pound boneless lamb, preferably leg

½ cup flour

Salt and pepper to taste

3 tablespoons olive oil

2 onions, peeled and chopped

2 carrots, peeled and sliced thinly

2 celery sticks, sliced finely

1 teaspoon smoked paprika

Pinch of cayenne pepper

2 pints water

½ stick butter, melted

2 tablespoons flour

¼ cup fresh lemon juice

A handful of fresh mint, chopped

Sour cream or plain yogurt for serving

Cut the lamb into fairly small chunks, not more than ¾ inch. Mix the flour with salt and pepper to taste and toss the lamb in this mixture. Warm the olive oil in the bottom of a large, deep stock pot, then fry the lamb chunks until just browned; add the onions, carrots, and celery, stir well, and sprinkle with paprika and cayenne. Add water and simmer for at least an hour or until the lamb is very soft. Remove any scum that rises to the top of the pot.

In a small bowl, combine the melted butter and 2 tablespoons flour to form a smooth paste. Gradually add this paste to the lamb mixture, simmering gently until the

soup thickens a little. Stir in the lemon juice and lastly the chopped fresh mint. Serve the soup in deep bowls topped with sour cream or plain yogurt.

Risotto Primavera

SERVES 4–6

Here's a simple springtime risotto recipe from Italy. As one of the seven sacred grains, rice is a powerful foodstuff on so many levels, bringing us peace, protection, and prosperity. Parsley, too, is a herb of both protection and spirituality. This can be made vegan by omitting butter and cheese (or using suitable vegetable-based products, such as more olive oil or vegan cheese) and using vegetable broth; you can also omit the wine and use more broth/water if you prefer, but the wine really adds a note of authenticity to this dish, and as we all know, the alcohol burns off in the cooking process.

>   4–5 cups vegetable or chicken broth
>   2 tablespoons each butter and olive oil
>   I medium onion, thinly sliced
>   Pinch of saffron
>   2 cups arborio or carnaroli rice
>   ¾ cup dry white wine
>   ½ cup fresh green peas
>   A handful fresh parsley, chopped
>   ¼ cup grated Parmesan cheese
>   Freshly ground black pepper

Heat the broth until hot but not boiling and set aside. In a large, deep saucepan, warm the butter and olive oil, then gently fry the onion until it is soft and golden. Stir in the saffron and then the rice, mixing gently to ensure it is coated with the oil and butter.

Gradually add the stock, ladle by ladle; stir until liquid is completely absorbed before adding the next ladle. This must be done slowly and carefully, and should take at least 30 to 45 minutes. When almost all the stock is absorbed into the rice, stir in the wine and green peas, and continue cooking for a few moments—there should be almost no liquid left in the pan. Sprinkle the risotto with the parsley, Parmesan, and black pepper to taste, and serve immediately in deep bowls.

Banoffee Pie

SERVES 8

Serve this traditional English dessert at teas or parties celebrating spring. The masculine energies of the bananas are full of life, fertility, and prosperity, the perfect offering at this time of new growth, and the cream and milk add a healthy mix of goddess and moon magic, too.

Preheat oven to 350°F. Butter a deep 9-inch pie plate well.

1½ cups graham cracker crumbs

1½ sticks butter, divided

1 large can sweetened condensed milk

½ cup dark brown sugar

1 teaspoon vanilla extract

½ teaspoon salt

3–4 large bananas

2 tablespoons lemon juice

1 cup heavy cream

1 tablespoon sugar

Melt ½ stick butter and mix with the graham cracker crumbs. Press this mixture evenly over the base of the pie plate and bake for 10 minutes. Cool.

In a large saucepan, combine the remaining butter, condensed milk, brown sugar, vanilla, and salt. Cook over low heat, stirring constantly, until the mixture forms a thick caramel. Cool. Peel and slice the bananas, sprinkle them with the lemon juice, and arrange them on the pie crust. Spread the cooled caramel carefully on top of the bananas. Whip the cream with the sugar until it forms soft peaks, then spread or pipe it on top of the caramel layer. Chill for 30 minutes before serving.

Quick Magic Seeded Bread

MAKES 1 LOAF

The name says it all: quick, delicious, and loaded with the positive auras of the seeds used, especially sesame seed, which is sacred in Hindu culture and also to the goddess Hecate. Sesame plants were believed to open gateways to the unknown and secret realms. The flours and grains used in this simple bread also bring grounding and peaceful energies. The recipe makes 1 medium loaf, but you can easily increase the quantities. Serve with soups, egg dishes, and colorful spring salads.

Preheat oven to 350°F. Butter a medium loaf pan very well.

> 3½ cups whole wheat flour
>
> ½ cup bran flakes
>
> 1 teaspoon baking powder
>
> 1 teaspoon salt
>
> 2 cups plain yogurt or buttermilk
>
> ¼ cup milk
>
> ¼ cup vegetable oil
>
> 2 tablespoons honey or molasses
>
> 1 cup chopped seeds (sesame, sunflower, pumpkin, etc.)

Sift the dry ingredients together in a large bowl. In a separate container, mix the yogurt, milk, oil, and honey together well, then stir into the dry ingredients. Beat together to form a batter. Stir in the seeds of your choice, keeping a few spoons of sesame seed aside. Spread the batter in the prepared baking pan and sprinkle with the additional seeds. Bake 45 to 50 minutes, then cool in the pans for 15 minutes before turning out onto a rack. Best eaten warm and fresh!

PANTRY

Lavender and Mint Conserve

MAKES ABOUT 1½ CUPS

Like an herbal honey, this fragrant conserve can be used in much the same way: added to baked goods, spread on scones or toast, or simply added to teas and other drinks, especially if you are feeling tired, scattered, or anxious in the spring season. Lavender calms and uplifts the spirit, and mint also has healing and purification qualities.

This recipe is adapted from one for rosemary conserve in Rachel Patterson's lovely book *A Kitchen Witch's World of Magical Food*.

> **1 cup fresh lavender flowers**
> **1 cup water**
> **A large handful fresh mint leaves**
> **2 cups sugar**
> **1 large lemon, juice and rind separated**

Place the lavender and water in a large saucepan and bring to a boil. Simmer gently for 5 minutes, then add the mint leaves and continue to simmer very slowly for a few more minutes. Remove from the heat and allow to cool.

When the liquid is cold, strain it back into the saucepan and add the sugar and the lemon juice and finely shredded lemon rind. Heat slowly until the sugar has dissolved, then boil rapidly for about 10 minutes—the liquid should start to thicken and have the consistency of syrup. Remove from heat and pour into a dry, sterilized jar when cold. Keep in a cool, dry place.

Four Thieves Vinegar

MAKES ABOUT 4 CUPS

There are actually many, many recipes for this vinegar, all claiming to be the original one that protected thieves and other miscreants from the plague in the Middle Ages. My recipe was given to me by an Italian friend; it is, as she told me, a very multi-purpose recipe, given that it can be added to all kinds of culinary creations like salads and sauces, while it is also suitable for use in cleaning and personal care recipes. It's healthy, joyful, and full of spring energy, however you choose to use it!

2 tablespoons fresh rosemary

2 tablespoons fresh thyme

2 bay leaves

2 tablespoons fresh oregano

2 whole cloves

4 cups white wine vinegar

Place the herbs and cloves in a large dry bottle or jar with a tight-fitting lid. Warm the vinegar until just simmering, then take off the heat and cool for 5 minutes. Pour it carefully over the herbs in the jar, cover, and leave for 2 weeks in a dark, cool place, shaking the bottle occasionally (if you remember). After this, strain the vinegar and discard the herbs and cloves. Store in small sterilized bottles and use within a month.

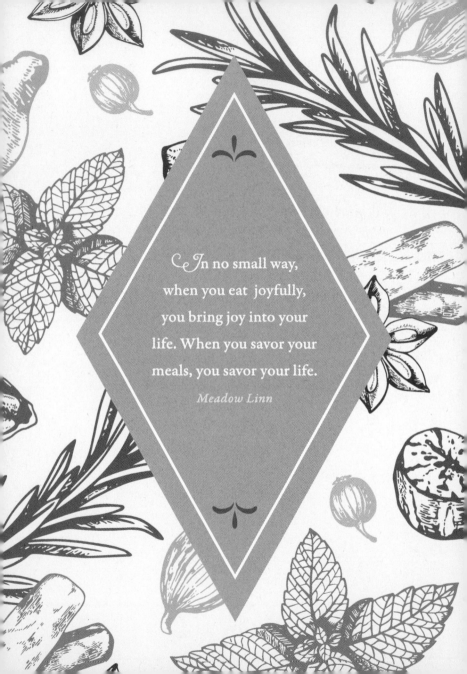

In no small way,
when you eat joyfully,
you bring joy into your
life. When you savor your
meals, you savor your life.

Meadow Linn

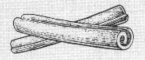

MAY

Passion and Joy

The magical month of May...a month when anything and everything seems possible! Of course, May 1 is Beltane in the Celtic calendar of the year, the day when love, fertility, and passion were celebrated in every way, much as the earth was ripening with the promise of summer to come.

This is a time for us to honor and celebrate our most passionate and sensual selves; sadly, this can still be something many of us, especially women, struggle with. As someone who was raised in an extremely conservative household where physical pleasure and sexuality were definitely not discussed and barely acknowledged, it took a long time for me to accept and appreciate my own sensuality on every level—and that includes the kitchen!

Actually, kitchens can be both passionate and erotic places—I have a friend who has moved home a number of times in the past few years, and she always takes her favorite kitchen table with her. But she says the kitchen is not really ready to be used until it has been consecrated by her and her partner making love on said table—I guess it certainly gives new meaning to the phrase "kitchen table magic." And don't forget that eating with your fingers, as well as feeding each other, can be a totally passionate affair!

When we truly enjoy the act of both cooking and eating, we are, of course, finding the joyful passion inherent in the most simple and basic of everyday activities, which is ultimately the true magic of life. Have you ever watched TV cooking shows? I love them, even if I don't watch them very often. However, there's a decided difference between the cooks and chefs featured on these shows: some simply prepare the food diligently and according to the recipe, and then there are those who really put their heart and soul into it. They love their ingredients, they love the process of preparation and cooking, and it shows! We become totally swept up in their magical carpet ride to culinary nirvana.

Love and passion are things we all need and want in our lives—without them we can live, obviously, but life is a pale version of what it could be. And that really can be changed starting in the kitchen—after all, earth gives us such amazing gifts and we, too, are so amazingly designed in our capacity to see, touch, taste, and celebrate these gifts on every level.

Becoming Our Own Love Goddess

There are many love gods and goddesses, and they all have something to offer us in their wisdom and beauty, but I believe we can actually best be our own love and passion gurus every day. Whether we are happily single, looking for a partner, or in a committed relationship, the real love story starts inside.

In your kitchen, gather a bunch of early summer roses (or even just one perfect bud); place it in a vase on the kitchen table. You will need your kitchen journal (or another journal if you prefer), too. Breathe in the soft scent of the roses—burn a rose-scented candle or incense if your rose is unscented. In your journal, write about the love you have now, the love you lost, the love you wish you had. Are you truly open to love, or—like so many of us—have you hardened and closed your heart because of past hurts and betrayals? The rose reminds us that we can be soft and

open, just like her petals, yet also maintain healthy and strong boundaries, as she does with her thorns.

Sit quietly with these thoughts for a while; think about a recipe that represents love to you, then write it down. (This could be a recipe you made or that someone else made for you—I always think about the bread that my partner made for me on the farm, the secret recipe that I ultimately stole from him with a kiss!) Perhaps you might like to make this recipe and savor it now, either alone or with someone you love. Look into the heart of the rose and quietly say these words:

> *Love is who I am. Love is with me and*
> *always will be. Love is my nourishment*
> *and my heart. Here and everywhere*
> *I choose love for myself, and I share love*
> *freely and with open hands. And so it is.*

Loving Spray Mist

This gentle yet powerful mist is a wonderful way to spice up your kitchen and yourself—plus any significant others sharing your space. Pour 1 cup boiling water over 2 chamomile tea bags in a small glass bowl; steep for 5 minutes, then strain the liquid and allow it to cool. Pour it into a spray bottle and add ½ cup witch hazel, 10 drops lavender essential oil, and 4 drops each lemongrass and vanilla

essential oils. Store in a cool, dark place and shake well before using. Don't spray in or near the eyes.

The Heartfelt Magic of Food

Obviously food is a central and essential part of our lives. Unfortunately, for many of us, it can also be a loaded issue, bringing up feelings of shame, guilt, anger, or resentment, which prevents us from wholeheartedly enjoying what we cook and eat. And while this is a book about creating kitchen enchantment and blessings, not about serious food issues that need to be addressed in other ways, I do believe we can all learn, as Meadow Linn says, to find joy in both our meals and our lives by changing our attitude to food.

I went through a stage of being quite overweight as a teenager, as so many girls do—and unfortunately there were those in my family who reminded me of it constantly, even in the context of teasing and pretending to be funny (when it wasn't). So I found it hard, for some years, to truly enjoy my own food (a little difficult when you work as a cook and baker) and often denied myself something I really would have enjoyed. It took a while, and some emotional breakthroughs, to realize that eating a brownie didn't make me bad; it made me human and normal.

Whatever our emotional triggers, we can learn to enjoy our food and allow it to bless us, not only for its nutritional

qualities but also on a deeper level. We can use it to lose limiting beliefs and blockages about who we are and what we truly deserve. And if there are particular foods or recipes that bring up painful thoughts or memories, it's time to let go of them—with love.

For a couple of years, I stopped making my favorite spicy chicken curry dish simply because it was the last meal I ever made for my partner before his sudden death. Making it just reminded me too much of that awful day. Then one day some friends asked me to make it for them, and I realized it was time to let go of this pain I had been holding on to. I got out my kitchen journal and prepared the chicken curry while writing down the thoughts and feelings that came up for me. I cried a little, laughed, and smiled as I went back through the memories of our relationship and how he loved this dish. Then I ate a little bowl of the curry and asked for blessings on myself and on his spirit.

So it can be with anything we make and eat: we can use it to bring us back to our present moment and sustain us on a new and joyful level. If there are any foods or recipes that you love but have been avoiding, this is a quiet little ritual that is often helpful. I do suggest that this one is best done alone.

First, gather the ingredients and utensils you need and place them on a table or countertop. Light a lavender

candle, then center and ground yourself, bare feet on the floor, and take a few deep breaths. Carefully and slowly prepare the recipe; while it is cooking/baking/chilling, stand in front of the candle and quietly say these words:

> *Food, you are life. You sustain me. I am so blessed to have food when others have none, this abundance for my body and hope for my life and heart. I remember meals from the past with love, gratitude, and peace. So, too, this meal today: it connects me to all who have brought this food to my plate and all those who have shared the story of my life, both now and in the past. My kitchen is a place of healing, abundance, and clarity for me and all those who come here. And so it is.*

Angels at My Kitchen Table

I believe in angels, in every possible way. Their presence is a constant support and comfort if we allow ourselves to be open to it. And I especially believe that they are always around, keeping us safe and happy, and trying (not always successfully) to keep us from making harmful choices. The love angels feel for us is a part of everything they do, and we don't have to go through elaborate rituals to conjure

them up: they're already there, unseen but definitely not unfelt in heart and soul.

I am particularly fond of my kitchen angel, who helps me with all my cooking efforts—even those that are less than wonderful. Actually, I believe she has been sent by those who originally taught me to cook (my mom and great-aunt) so many years ago, to oversee what I am up to these days with the pots and pans. And I definitely think my better kitchen creations and moments of inspiration are down to my kitchen angel's guidance. On days when I really feel low and depleted—with no energy for cooking or, indeed, anything else—I sense her gentle presence and support telling me that it's okay to just keep it simple and relax.

Angels are part of every spiritual tradition and belief system through time. Although they sometimes look different and have different names, they are basically all part of the same divine and magical network, and they can take any form you choose. (I love the movie *Ratatouille*, where Remy, the cooking rat, has a kitchen angel in the form of the decidedly rotund Chef Gusteau!)

I often find a white feather on my kitchen floor in the morning, and there is no way a bird could have left it there overnight. I take this as a beautiful sign of my kitchen angel's presence and always make a point of saying thank

you. Angels in general like white, so white candles and flowers are always welcome, as are crystals like quartz, amethyst, and selenite. I also have a simple bead-and-wire angel figure that hangs up in my kitchen window; she turns a little with the breeze and almost seems to be alive—which, of course, in a very real sense, she is.

Honor your kitchen angel with your thanks and gratitude; maybe even make an ethereal angel food cake or angel-shaped cookies once in a while. Use fragrances that angels enjoy, either as scented candles or incense—frankincense, vanilla, jasmine, neroli, rose, or sandalwood are among their favorites. And in your kitchen journal, keep a note of any messages you receive from them.

Always before a meal or when saying grace, we should remember to thank the angels for their help, not only in our kitchens and cooking, but in our lives in general. After eating and at night before leaving the kitchen, thank them again for their presence and support.

The Fragrant Kitchen

The truly delicious kitchen has its own wonderful aromas. Is there anything nicer than the scent of vanilla and spices from a fruit cake baking in the oven or the taste-tingling aroma of onions and garlic frying in a pan and holding the promise of a wonderful dinner to come?

Although we tend to associate aromatherapy more with health, beauty, and bathroom rituals, there is also a place for it in kitchen magic, particularly when the energies of the kitchen (and those who work or eat in it) feel depleted and negative. There are many ways to introduce the magic of essential oils in your kitchen space—my personal favorite is adding them to the kitchen candles, which we have already talked about (see page 17). While it is possible to buy all sorts of scented candles these days, some with truly weird and wonderful fragrance combinations, I prefer to use plain white candles and simply add a few drops of the chosen essential oil to the well that forms around the wick of the candle. (Do this carefully and slowly, and be sure not to pour oil directly onto the burning wick.)

Diffusers and oil burners can also be used in this way. Ensure that they are always in a safe place away from naked heat and where they cannot be knocked over, especially if there are children or pets around.

Here are some fragrance ideas for your kitchen; you can use them singly or try them in combinations:

- If you want to feel energized and have better focus and concentration in your kitchen, try rosemary, thyme, lemon, or peppermint oil.

- For a peaceful and tranquil kitchen environment, lavender, rose, chamomile, neroli, and sandalwood oils are recommended.

- After a tense or difficult period, or when there have been arguments in the kitchen, find harmony again with geranium, lavender, patchouli, or orange.

- When your kitchen feels hot and frankly less than fragrant, a blend of lemon, lemon verbena, and rosemary oils will immediately give it a fresh and clean feeling.

- When you or others who share your kitchen are just feeling blue, try lemongrass, basil, and jasmine oils.

Kitchen Pleasures

- Brew a cup of dandelion tea using fresh flower heads that you have gathered and rinsed. You will find this bright, sunny, and tenacious little plant gives you new hope and allows you to open up to guiding spirits in your life. You can also use dandelion roots and leaves in salads and other culinary creations. Remember that dandelion flowers can also be dried and kept to add a little sunshine to the winter months.

- Mix some pumpkin, sesame, and sunflower seeds together in a blender to form a powder. Sprinkle this nutritious and magical mix over baked goods, cereals, vegetables, and salads.

- May 23 is the Feast of the Madonna in Italy. Honoring the Mother Goddess, this is a special time for cleaning and blessing our kitchens. Prepare recipes that use ingredients sacred to her, such as apples, eggs, tomatoes, mushrooms, milk, cream, honey, and roses.

- Practice *Gokotta*—a Swedish tradition which means "early rising cuckoo." Sit in your kitchen in the early morning—preferably with the windows and doors open—and enjoy all the sounds of the early summer.

RECIPES

Creamy Garlic Soup

SERVES 4

A soup for passion and awakening the senses—and, surprisingly, it is not overpoweringly flavored by the garlic. Roasting garlic gives it a subtle and mellow sweetness; it works wonderfully well with the thyme, too. Garlic was originally thought to inspire lust and desire—even if it did nothing for the breath—but I prefer to see this soup as a wonderful way of creating positive energies in this beautiful time of early summer, while at the same time protecting us from anything that might undermine these good things.

Preheat oven to 200°F.

> **2 tablespoons olive oil**
> **4 fresh bulbs of garlic, divided**
> **4 cups chicken or vegetable broth**
> **A few sprigs of fresh thyme**
> **1 cup light cream**

½ cup grated Parmesan

Freshly ground black pepper

Spread the olive oil on a small baking sheet, and place three of the garlic bulbs on it. Roast, uncovered, for 25 minutes, then remove from the heat and leave to cool.

Heat the broth in a saucepan, then add the crushed cloves of the remaining bulb of garlic. Add the thyme leaves that you have stripped off the branches. Simmer for 10 minutes. Stir in the cream, then add the softened garlic pulp that you have squeezed out of the roasted garlic heads. Simmer very gently for another 10 minutes, then remove from the heat and puree the soup (a stick blender works well for this). Return to the heat and stir in the Parmesan and black pepper to taste.

Serve the soup hot in small cups or bowls, with lots of fresh bread for dipping. You can also add a garnish of more finely chopped thyme leaves.

Chicken and Prawn Paella

SERVES 6

Quite a festive dish, this paella is suitable for sharing with others in this month of love and passion. It's a slightly simplified version of the traditional Spanish paella, which requires lots of ingredients and a special paella pan, too. The shrimp, chicken, chorizo, and clams (or mussels) are all traditional to this dish, but you can swap out any of them to suit personal preference. The rice that forms the basis of this dish is both grounding and comforting, and the saffron is a powerful healing spice with lots of joyful energy.

Preheat oven to 325°F.

½ teaspoon saffron threads

¼ cup olive oil

6–8 chicken thighs or breasts, skin on

2 onions, finely chopped

2 garlic cloves, crushed

1 red pepper, seeded and chopped

1 large chorizo sausage, sliced

1½ cups white rice

4 cups hot chicken stock, divided

½ cup dry white wine

1 large can crushed tomatoes

Salt and pepper to taste

¼ cup butter

8 ounces shrimp, deveined

¼ cup fresh lemon juice

1 teaspoon smoked paprika

4 ounces clams in shells

½ cup green peas

Lemon slices

Handful of fresh parsley, chopped

Soak the saffron threads in a tablespoon of hot water and set aside. Warm the olive oil in a large frying pan and fry the chicken pieces until golden brown. Remove from the oil and keep warm. In the same pan, fry the onions, garlic, red pepper, and sliced chorizo until the vegetables are softened. Stir in the rice and toss to coat it with the oil. Stir in 3 cups of the chicken stock and wine, then add the tomatoes. Salt and pepper to taste.

Spread this mixture in a large casserole dish and place the chicken pieces on top. Cover the dish and bake in the preheated oven for an hour—after this, the rice should be soft and the liquid absorbed. Add the remaining chicken stock and the reserved saffron liquid and continue to bake for another 30 minutes or so. The chicken should be very tender.

While this is happening, warm the butter in a frying pan, and add the shrimp together with the lemon juice and

smoked paprika; stir fry the shrimp until just cooked, then stir in the clams and continue to cook until the shells open; discard any that remain closed. Add the shrimp and clam mixture to the chicken and rice, arranging them on top. (If the mixture seems dry, add a little more stock, water, or wine.) Cover the dish and heat through for about 20 minutes. Remove from the heat and add the peas. Serve at once with lemon wedges and sprinkled with lots of fresh parsley.

Persian Love Cake

MAKES 1 CAKE FOR 10–12 SERVINGS

We all know that love spells can be tricky and sometimes backfire—particularly if they violate the principle of free will—but I venture to suggest that this unusual and subtly flavored cake would be a good way to get someone interested in you! This recipe has its origins in ancient Persian folklore, when a rather ordinary young girl used it to make a handsome young prince fall in love with her.

There are also versions of this cake to be found in other parts of the Middle and Far East too, but wherever it comes from, the basic principles of love, affection, and passion are reflected in the flavorings of cardamom (one of my favorite spices) and rose. Warming and uplifting, the crushed seeds also bring protection and clarity to you and your home. And the addition of semolina, again often

122

used in Mediterranean and Middle Eastern cooking, adds a different dimension of taste and texture to this soft and delicious cake.

Heat oven to 350°F. Grease a 9-inch square baking pan.

1 stick butter, softened
1 cup sugar
3 eggs, separated
½ cup plain yogurt
1 tablespoon rose water
Grated zest of 1 lime or lemon
1 cup flour
1 cup fine semolina
2 teaspoons baking powder
1 teaspoon ground cardamom seed

Cream the butter and sugar together well; then beat in 3 egg yolks, yogurt, rose water, and lime or lemon zest. Sift together the flour, semolina, baking powder, and ground cardamom, then fold into the butter mixture to form a smooth batter. Lastly, beat the 3 egg whites until fluffy and soft and fold them gently into the batter. Pour the mixture into the pan and bake for 45 to 50 minutes or until the cake is light golden brown and risen.

Rose Syrup
While the cake is baking, make the rose syrup by combining ½ cup each sugar and water in a small saucepan and

heating until the sugar is completely dissolved. Stir in 1 teaspoon rose water and a pinch of ground cardamom.

Remove the cake from the oven and spoon the warm syrup over it, allowing it to soak in. Cool and then cut into small squares to serve; a few fresh rose petals make a beautiful garnish, and in some recipes crushed pistachio nuts are also sprinkled over the cake.

Faery Truffles
MAKES 20–30 TRUFFLES

We all know faeries love sweet little offerings, so if you want to keep in their good books and ensure their continued magical help in your kitchen, might I suggest these simple little unbaked treats? Leave a few out overnight on your kitchen altar and there will definitely be some happy faeries living in your home. This recipe is also vegan if agave syrup or coconut sugar replaces the honey, and it's easy enough for children to make; I usually place each of the truffles in a little silver paper cup and top each one with a little dried rose petal or lavender sprig for a delightful springtime gift.

> 1½ cups rolled oats (not instant)
> 1 cup ground almonds
> ½ cup organic coconut oil
> ½ cup raw honey
> ½ cup unsweetened cocoa

1 teaspoon vanilla extract
Chopped nuts/coconut

Mix the oats and ground almonds together in a bowl. Over low heat, melt the coconut oil and honey together, then stir in the cocoa to form a smooth mixture. Add the vanilla. Remove from the heat and stir in the oats/almonds—you may not need to use all of this, as you want a mixture that is soft but can still be molded with your hands. Form the mixture into small balls (about ¾ inch in diameter is ideal) and place in small paper cups to set. If it's fairly warm in your kitchen, they should be placed in the refrigerator.

Magical Mystery Salt

MAKES ABOUT 1¼ CUPS

I love making flavored salts for use in both the kitchen and magical spells and rituals—the possibilities are literally endless, and you can make your own combinations of favorite herbs and spices. This is one of my own favorite salt blends, which I use liberally in all kinds of cooking, from barbecues to sauces and marinades. You can also use this mixture to fill small protection or blessing bags, or place a little in bowls around the kitchen to ensure good mojo and happy vibes.

First, peel a large lemon and cut the peel into strips. Bake the strips at 325°F for 30 minutes or until the peel is crisp. Cool, then crumble into small pieces. Place 1 cup sea salt in a glass bowl. Stir in the lemon rind pieces, then add 1 teaspoon each paprika, cayenne pepper, dill, ground black pepper, garlic powder, and ground coriander. Mix well and store in small glass jars in a cool, dark place.

Sweet Hand Scrub

Although this looks and smells almost good enough to eat, this simple scrub is something I like to keep on my pantry shelf, especially during summer, to use on hands that feel hot, irritated, or just plain grimy. It also works well on hands and feet that are less than happy after time spent in the garden. The lavender is, of course, both calming and uplifting, and the tea tree oil works to ease any little irritations or infections.

> 1½ cups brown sugar
> ½ cup sweet almond or jojoba oil
> 10 drops lavender essential oil
> 8 drops tea tree essential oil
> 2 teaspoons glycerin
> Dried lavender flowers (optional)

Place the brown sugar in a large glass bowl and stir in the sweet almond or jojoba oil, then add the essential oils and mix well. Stir in the glycerin and, if you are using them, a handful of crushed lavender flowers. Place the scrub in small glass jars and keep in a cool, dry place. To use, scoop out a handful of the scrub and rub it gently all over your hands. Rinse off well with cool water.

There are always flowers
for those who want to see them.

Henri Matisse

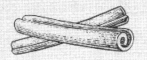

JUNE

Celebrating All That Is Green and Blooming

The summer solstice (in the northern hemisphere)—traditionally known as Litha—occurs around June 21 and marks the point of the sun's greatest power and strength. At this time in the far north it almost never gets dark at all; I spent a few months living in the far north of Scotland a few years ago and could not believe the almost constant light. As someone who doesn't much like the darkness, it was a truly magical time and one I will never forget.

The summer solstice has been marked by traditional ceremonies down through the centuries, with the most celebrated one being simply gathering together to watch the sunrise on this day and marking it by coming together to feast and enjoy the bright warmth given to us by Mother Earth. Certainly June as a whole should be the month when we spend as much time as possible outside, and we can also bring the outside into our kitchens and homes by choosing to lighten up wherever possible—sheer drapes and curtains, for example, as well as in the food and cooking choices we make. Think light, raw, fresh—or simple, minimal one-dish meals using the many abundant fruits, vegetables, and herbs available to us at this time.

It's time to enjoy and savor early summer's bounty; if possible, take time to gather or forage some wild plants (ensuring that you know what you are collecting and also that it is permissible for you to do so). In this way we can learn the real "roots" of the food we eat. Spicy dishes are also a good idea at this time, for it's no coincidence that many of the hottest climates in the world are also home to the spiciest of foods. Spicy foods help us perspire, which is the most natural form of cooling.

With its bright and blossoming promise, Litha also reminds us to look at what is blossoming and growing in our own lives. Are we tending our inner gardens well, and

130

are they bringing forth the colors and brightness we long for? How can we use this warm and fragrant season to best help us grow in joy and grace? These are all questions that Litha can help us answer if we are open to the magic of this time.

The Flowers of Blodeuedd

Blodeuedd—the name means "flower face" or "born of flowers"—is, like Airmid, not generally seen as a kitchen goddess, although she is linked to the earth as well as the flowers that inspired her name. But I feel she's a beautiful goddess for the summer, and in particular the blossoming month of June, and as such she deserves a place in our kitchens and hearts.

In Celtic legend she was actually conjured out of flowers by the magicians Gwydion and Math to become the wife of Gwydion's nephew, Lleu, and was reputed to be the most beautiful woman in the world. But, as so often happens, she fell in love with someone else: Goronwy; she and her lover plotted the death of her husband, Lleu, but he was saved by the two magicians, who then turned Blodeuedd into an owl, the bird of the night, presumably in revenge.

Later in this section you will find some ideas for cooking with and using flowers in your kitchen, all of which can be a tribute to this beautiful, if entirely human, goddess.

131

Even just simply placing a small vase or jug of fresh flowers on the kitchen table reminds us of beauty, grace, and the brief glory that is summer.

The Zero-Waste Kitchen

As hearth and kitchen witches, we choose a path that not only follows the patterns of our earth and her seasons, but also works in harmony with it on several levels. Part of this is done by showing respect to the earth and her gifts with the choices we make on a daily basis—choices that hopefully support nature on every level. Anything else is just not an option, especially at this moment in time, when centuries of human abuse and neglect have taken such a heavy toll on this beautiful planet we call home and wreaked havoc on the soil, the trees, the oceans and rivers, the weather patterns, and even the very air we breathe.

As part of the enchanted kitchen journey, we can do small, incremental things and make healthier choices. This may sometimes seem too little, too late—but if we all commit to this, we will start to see a shift back to a healing and healthier world for everyone.

This starts with everyday choices we make in our kitchens and homes: something as simple as choosing to buy fruit and vegetables at our local summer food markets, rather than buying shrink-wrapped products imported

from who knows where, at what cost to both quality and the environment. This ensures we are not only supporting local entrepreneurship but eating something a lot fresher and more sustainable. As an example: I used to buy small frozen potato gratins, which I later realized were actually imported from Belgium, something reflected in the fairly high price. Yes, they were convenient, but was it actually that much more difficult to buy local potatoes and make a batch of my own little potato dishes to store in the freezer? No.

Other ideas for turning your magical kitchen into a low-waste zone:

- As already said, try to buy fresh, local, and in season wherever possible; if possible, grow your own. There really is nothing like harvesting your own herbs and vegetables, even if you do have to figure out what to do with those piles of zucchini or green beans and your neighbors are starting to avoid you!

- Cut down on or eliminate the use of chemical cleaning products in your kitchen and the rest of your home. It's just so simple to make your own, using ingredients you probably already have on your kitchen shelf. (See page 89 for some ideas.)

- Choose glass jars and bottles, not plastic, wherever practically possible. A bonus is that, although glass may be a little more expensive initially, it can be used, washed, and reused countless times. (In fact, I choose glass for just about everything in my kitchen, from bowls to oven dishes.)

- Bamboo is another wonderful choice for kitchen utensils and the like—bowls, steamers, chopping boards, even bamboo straws!

- This probably hardly needs to be said, but choose reusable fabric bags for shopping—as we all know, plastic shopping bags are right up there at the top of the "plastic problem." The same applies to the cloths you use in your kitchen for cleaning and drying. Paper towels are handy in the kitchen, but try to limit their use.

- Try to throw away as little food as possible—this is not only horribly wasteful, but it goes against the whole concept of supporting the earth and all who live on it. Discover new ways of pickling, bottling, and storing fresh fruits, vegetables, and herbs; you'll find some ideas in the pantry section for each month. If you really have food items

such as vegetables that are unusable because of mold and the like, consider starting a compost bin or simply returning them to the earth. Turn stale bread into breadcrumbs (they keep well in the freezer) and use as a topping on casseroles, for fried chicken, and more.

- ◆ Extra fresh herbs can be chopped finely and placed in ice cube trays with a little water and olive oil, to be added to dishes as needed. You can do this with lemon zest and juice as well.

Beeswax Wraps

I grew up in an age when plastic wrap was the absolute go-to wrapping material in the kitchen—everything was plastic-wrapped to within an inch of its life! Hopefully we know a little better now; after all, it's perfectly possible to simply put a plate on top of a bowl! Another alternative that is becoming increasingly popular are beeswax wraps, and it's fairly easy to make your own. Naturally antibacterial, these wraps can be wiped clean if necessary and reused a number of times.

Melt beeswax in a wide, shallow bowl over a pan of simmering water. Measure the bowls you will want to cover and cut a piece of suitable fabric (cotton or thick muslin)

into a circle, adding a few inches all round. Dip the fabric into the melted beeswax and ensure it's saturated on both sides. Remove and let it dry on a piece of wax paper. (The wraps should be stored on wax paper in a cool place, never near a heat source or in direct sunlight.) To use, simply use the warmth of your hands to mold and shape the wrap over the bowl or other dish you are covering. After use, flatten out, wipe clean if needed, and store flat until you need to use it again.

Flower Energies in the Kitchen

Flowers are not generally as widely used in the kitchen as, for example, herbs, spices, fruits, or vegetables, but they have an important role to play in the enchanted kitchen on several levels: taste, beauty, inspiration, and healing. Like all growing things, flowers possess their own unique energies, and the knowledge of this is as old as the culinary arts themselves. For example, both roses and orange blossoms have been used in the cuisines of the Middle East for centuries. And in the early summer months, when the garden is at its brightest and most beautiful, what better time to enjoy these very special gifts of the earth?

The ways in which flower energies can be used in the kitchen are diverse. They can be added to culinary preparations like drinks, cakes, and desserts or chopped and sprin-

kled on salads and other cold dishes for a burst of vibrant color. Flower fragrances can be added to food in the form of culinary rose water, for example, or we can simply allow their gentle scent to become part of our kitchen through adding a few drops of essential oil to burners or diffusers or scented candles or incense. In general, light and spicy fragrances work best in the kitchen, particularly in the warm summer months: for example, rose, lavender, vanilla, rosemary, or neroli.

The unique and potent energies of flowers are also wonderful when used as flower essences. It's easy to make your own; see page 261 of my book *Enchanted Herbal*. Because flower essences are completely natural and nontoxic, a few drops can be added to liquids when cooking or baking or stirred into cool drinks.

However, it's also important to remember that not all flowers are nontoxic when used in their natural state of blossom and petal—in fact, some are highly poisonous! The ones listed below are all safe to use, but if you are in doubt, consult your local plant center for advice. It's also not generally a good idea to use flowers from a florist, which are often treated in some way to preserve color/ life; if at all possible, use freshly picked flowers from your own (or someone else's garden—ask first!), and never use flowers picked from the side of busy roads since they

unfortunately will also have picked up pollution and other nasties.

Some beautiful and magical flowers to use in your cooking include the following. This is not a complete list by any means; I am just giving you some ideas for flowers that are generally fairly easy to find and grow.

CARNATION: like chrysanthemum, another bright and beautiful flower to be sprinkled liberally on cold dishes for the simple enjoyment of life and the healing of heartache and grief (one of the reasons carnations have long been used at funerals and memorial services).

CHRYSANTHEMUM: a flower that has long been used in the Far and Middle East, not only for traditional rituals and ceremonies, but also in the kitchen, where its bright and peppery petals can be added to salads and used as a garnish for other dishes. This flower has the energies of protection, longevity, and helping to heal fear of the future or the unknown.

FREESIA: such a beautiful plant, with an unforgettable fragrance; the flowers can be strewn on dishes and baked goods. Steep a few blossoms in water overnight, then strain and

use the liquid in baked goods for a delicate touch of summer flavor. Freesia is known for helping to ease depression; it helps on those days when everything just seems like too much effort. This lovely flower brings new clarity and purpose for the future; however, it should always be remembered that serious depression needs professional medical help.

GERANIUM: use the fragrant petals as a garnish, add them to desserts, or use the petals when creating syrups and summery drinks. Geranium is a grounding and nurturing plant, offering safety and strength to the home and those who dwell therein.

HONEYSUCKLE: the lovely, fragrant flowers can be used in similar ways to freesia; a simple cake made with honeysuckle water added to the batter is truly amazing. The emotional energies of honeysuckle are pretty powerful too: abundance, prosperity, better health, releasing blocks, and moving forward to new beginnings.

LAVENDER: the dried or chopped fresh blossoms make a wonderful addition to so many dishes— and not just baked goods, as is often presumed.

Try adding a few crumbled lavender flowers to salad dressings or sauces, or make a lavender butter with lemon and a little mint to spread on grilled meat or chicken. Scatter a few dried blossoms in a jug of iced tea or a sparkling wine punch ... the possibilities are endless with this lovely herb. Remember to use lavender in moderation since it can be a little overwhelming in flavor. And we use lavender as a spiritual and healing herb in so many ways—for peace, protection, cleansing, and positivity.

MARIGOLD (CALENDULA): such a pretty and sunny flower; one just feels brighter looking at it! Give your salads and sauces an infusion of color with a sprinkling of marigold petals or add them to milk or cream when making custard-type sauces—this is a very old way of using the petals to add not only flavor but a lovely golden color to the finished dish. Marigold is a flower for well-being, fidelity, happiness, and the healing of old and unhelpful patterns, whether emotional or physical.

NASTURTIUM: this was one of my late mother's favorite flowers, and she almost always had a small jug of these bright flowers on the kitchen table. The flowers and leaves add a distinct peppery tang to all sorts of dishes, and the seeds can also be pickled and used as a substitute for capers. I particularly like nasturtiums as a garnish for rice dishes or green salads. These are happiness flowers, making life just seem that much better in so many ways.

PANSIES & VIOLETS (ALL MEMBERS OF THE VIOLA FAMILY): often candied and used on baked goods, they can also be added to salads or used as a garnish on other dishes. They are known for their bright beauty that brings fresh energy and perspective when we feel overwhelmed by daily tasks and commitments; they remind us to slow down and enjoy the simple joys of the moment.

ROSE: use in desserts, baking, candies, and as a garnish for just about anything. Rose energy protects and blesses your kitchen in a particularly beautiful and sacred way; it also strengthens bonds of friendship and love and creates a positive and protective aura.

Kitchen Pleasures

- Go nuts! In the warm summer months, we probably don't want or need to cook as much, and eating raw foods is both more pleasant and also healthful. Nuts represent a powerful package of health in a very tasty form, so always try to keep a bowl of nuts around for snacking. All of these are particularly tasty, either individually or in combination: hazelnuts, cashews, almonds, macadamias, pecans, and Brazil nuts—which, by the way, are actually a complete protein, as they contain all nine essential amino acids.

- Make a scented splash for yourself or to sprinkle in your kitchen as both cleanser and benediction: mix 1 cup vodka with 6 whole cardamom seeds and 6 drops each neroli, geranium, and lemon essential oils. Allow to steep for a few weeks, then strain and add 1 cup spring water. Store it in a mister or spray bottle.

- Gather fresh mint, marjoram, or oregano on Midsummer Eve, and dry it for use in recipes and rituals later in the year.

- Experiment with a fruit you haven't used before: add it to a smoothie or herbal water, or make a beautiful and colorful fruit salad (see the August chapter for more magical correspondences linked to fruit).

RECIPES

Avocado Magic

Avocados have to be one of the most inherently magical fruits around, and they're certainly amongst the oldest; evidence of their existence dates back millennia. They have been sacred to many cultures, most notably the Mayans and Aztecs, who believed the avocado was an aphrodisiac that also enhanced fertility—well, I suppose the two things do really go hand in hand. Just cutting open an avocado to reveal that smooth and buttery green flesh surrounding the dark and secretive stone is a kind of magic all in itself.

I grew up in a garden with lots of avocado trees so they were always in abundance in our kitchen, but I also learned that, in general, keeping it simple was the best way to treat these magical gifts of the earth. So, here are two fairly easy recipes for summer days:

Avocado Cream

Cut a perfectly ripe avocado in half and remove the stone. Scoop the flesh out into a bowl and add a little salt, ¼ cup plain or coconut yogurt, 2 tablespoons fresh lemon juice, and 1 tablespoon olive oil. Blend together very well to form a thick, creamy green puree. Serve chilled with breads, salads, grilled fish or meat…just about anything!

Spicy Avocado Salad

Peel two ripe avocados, remove the stones, and cut into small dice. Place in a serving bowl. Gently stir in 1 small finely chopped red onion, 1 teaspoon crushed garlic, and a handful of finely chopped cilantro (coriander) leaves. Add 2 tablespoons fresh lemon juice and a few drops hot sauce. Toss all together well, then place in the refrigerator to chill. Serve on the day it is made.

Ginger and Honey Baked Pork Chops
SERVES 6

A fragrant and deliciously simple main course for summer, this can also be adapted for chicken pieces or lamb chops and is lovely cooked on a barbecue. Enjoy the healing and magical properties of the ginger and the happiness power inherent in honey as you make and eat this dish.

2 pounds lamb chops

2 garlic cloves, crushed

2 tablespoons crushed fresh ginger

2 tablespoons soy sauce

¼ cup honey

½ cup white wine (or sherry)

1 tablespoon brown sugar

Salt and pepper to taste

Chopped fresh sage for garnish

Preheat oven to 325°F.

Remove excess fat or rind from the pork chops and arrange them in a single layer in a large glass or ceramic baking dish. Mix together all the remaining ingredients, apart from the fresh sage, and pour this evenly over the chops. If you like, leave the meat to marinate for 1 hour; however, this isn't essential.

Cover the dish and bake for 1 hour or until the meat is soft and cooked. Remove the covering and continue to bake for another 30 minutes, by which time the sauce should be reduced and thick. Sprinkle with chopped fresh sage and serve hot.

Summer Vegetable Couscous

SERVES 4–6

A light and lovely main dish, couscous is actually not a grain but a very, very fine pasta made from semolina wheat. It makes a good substitute for ordinary pasta or rice in the hot summer months. You can, of course, add all sorts of things to this dish—swap out the parsley for mint, stir in chopped olives, feta cheese, and more—but I generally like to keep it simple so the fresh flavors of the vegetables stand out. The dish should be served warm on a large serving platter, garnished with lemon wedges and some additional chopped parsley.

2 tablespoons butter

2 tablespoons olive oil

1 large red pepper, cut into strips

1 large onion, finely sliced

1 clove garlic, crushed

1 cup shredded zucchini

¼ cup chopped fresh parsley

¼ cup lemon juice

1 teaspoon dried oregano

1½ cups chicken or vegetable broth

½ teaspoon salt

1 cup uncooked couscous

Lemon wedges and chopped parsley for garnish

Heat the butter and oil in a large frying pan and fry the red pepper for a few minutes; then stir in the onion, garlic, and zucchini and continue frying until the vegetables are just tender. Remove from the heat and stir in the parsley, lemon juice, and oregano.

While the vegetables are cooking, mix warmed broth with salt and then stir in the couscous, stirring well with a fork until the liquid is absorbed and the couscous is light and fluffy. Add the couscous to the warm vegetables and mix together lightly before spooning the mixture onto the serving platter.

Cheese Creams with Strawberry Puree

MAKES 6

Light and delicate, these soft and creamy little desserts are a fitting end to a summer feast. On a magical note, I once prepared these for a relative stranger who was coming to dinner—and, quite unexpectedly, that stranger became the love of my life, so perhaps the strawberries lived up to their reputation as fruits for igniting love and passion. Cheese, too, is linked with love in all its forms, so basically you can't go wrong with this pretty dish.

1 tablespoon gelatin

3 tablespoons cold water

8 ounces soft cream cheese

¼ cup sugar

1 teaspoon vanilla extract

1 egg, separated

½ cup heavy cream

1½ cups chopped fresh strawberries

1 teaspoon lemon juice

2 tablespoons sugar

Strawberries and mint leaves for garnish

Soak the gelatin in the cold water and set aside. Beat the cream cheese with the sugar, vanilla, and egg yolk. Dissolve the gelatin over a jug of boiling water, then fold into the cream cheese mixture. Beat the egg white until stiff, then gently mix into the cream cheese, followed by the cream, also beaten to soft peaks. Chill the mixture in the refrigerator until it has the texture of a soft mousse.

To make the strawberry puree, mix the chopped strawberries with the lemon juice and sugar, then blend or mash, adding enough water to make a fairly thick puree. To serve, place scoops of the cream cheese mousse on small plates, then surround with the strawberry puree. Garnish with additional small strawberries or fresh mint leaves.

The Beautiful Cake

SERVES 8–10

So it was named by a friend of mine, and so it will always be—a deceptively simple and light cake made beautiful by its subtle floral flavoring and also by the flowers that surround and garnish it. (For a list of suitable flowers, see page 138.) I use jasmine tea bags when making this cake, but you could use other flavors: chamomile, rose petal, or even a lavender tea infusion. This cake has a simple cream filling and topping—rich, sweet frostings tend to overpower the delicate flavor.

Preheat oven to 350°F. Grease two 8- or 9-inch cake pans well.

> ½ cup boiling water
>
> 2 jasmine tea bags
>
> 4 eggs, separated
>
> 1 cup sugar
>
> 1 teaspoon vanilla extract
>
> 1 cup flour
>
> 1½ tablespoons cornstarch
>
> 2 teaspoons baking powder
>
> ½ teaspoon salt

Pour the boiling water over the tea bags in a cup or mug, steep for 10 minutes, then remove the bags and allow the liquid to cool. Place the egg yolks in a large bowl and beat in the cold tea, sugar, and vanilla to make a thick and creamy mixture. Sift together the flour and other dry ingredients, then fold into the egg yolk mixture. Beat the egg whites in a grease-free glass bowl until they are stiff but not dry and gently fold them in. Pour the batter into the two prepared cake pans, leveling with a spatula, and bake in the preheated oven for 10 to 15 minutes or until cakes are well risen and test done. To test done simply insert a metal or wooden skewer into the thicker part of the cake; if it comes out without sticky batter adhering to it, it is done. Turn out onto a wire rack and allow to cool.

For the filling, beat 1½ cups heavy cream until soft peaks form, then gradually add 2 tablespoons sugar and 1 teaspoon vanilla extract. Place one cake layer on the serving dish or cake plate and spread with half of the cream. Place the other cake on top and swirl the remaining cream over the surface. Garnish beautifully with edible flowers; you can also add a garland around the base of the cake. Keep chilled until just before serving.

Rose Calming Oil

For many of us, roses are the epitome of beauty, fragrance, and grace. They hold so much power within their scented petals and are known for their ability to impart a sense of peace, well-being, and happiness. We are used to them being used in various beauty preparations, of course, but it's also possible to bring their fabulous vibe into our kitchens anytime we need a little boost of heart and spirit.

This is a very simple preparation that can be kept in a glass jar and simply used whenever necessary. You will need ½ cup sweet almond oil, 10 drops rose essential oil, and 5 drops lavender oil. Mix them together well and pour into your chosen jar. (You can stick a few dried rosebuds on the lid of the jar for an even prettier effect!) Keep the jar on a shelf in the kitchen that is away from direct heat and sunlight, and simply rub a few drops onto your hands, base of the throat, or temples anytime you feel a little tired or stressed in the kitchen.

Marinated Olives

This is not really a precise recipe; it's more some suggestions for creating your own flavored olive combinations according to personal taste and what you have in your garden or kitchen. Seasoned olives are a staple of the enchanted pantry and add a little magical flair to just about anything—even something as simple as a plate of cheese and crackers. Basically, you need to start with about 8 ounces black or green olives, preferably packed in brine. Rinse well (otherwise they will be too salty) and place in a bowl. Add ¾ cup olive oil (or enough to cover the olives) and then stir in your chosen flavorings, which could include thinly sliced peel of orange or lemon, peeled garlic cloves cut into thin slices, 1 tablespoon green or black peppercorns, chili flakes, crushed coriander or cardamom seeds, a couple of bay leaves, and a tablespoon of chopped fresh herbs such as rosemary or thyme.

Allow the mixture to stand for a day so that the flavors can infuse, then store the jar in the refrigerator. The olives will keep for a couple of weeks. You can also top up the jar with more oil so the olives don't become dry.

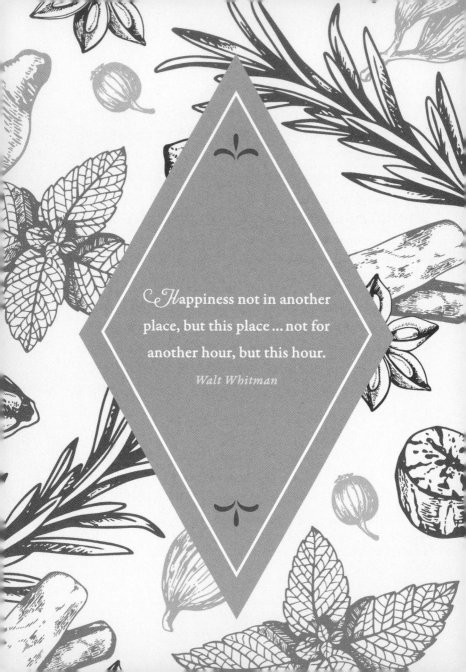

Happiness not in another place, but this place ... not for another hour, but this hour.

Walt Whitman

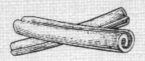

JULY

Abundance and Color

July is the very height of summer and usually a time of natural vibrance, color, and sunshine. It's also often a time when we are on vacation and enjoying a break from our usual routines. For this reason, July should also be a time of stepping back physically and emotionally and for keeping things very simple—especially in the kitchen.

This is not the time for elaborate or time-consuming recipes—eat fresh plant-based meals wherever and whenever possible. As summer starts to come towards her end, we also start to think ahead and plan for the future as we

move into fall and winter. Everything is bright and bloom-
ing now, so how do we plan to carry that warmth with us?
How can we keep the promise of this beautiful season alive
in our hearts and lives? These are questions summer asks of
us, and hopefully we will find creative and joyful answers
in this month. Enjoy and celebrate our lives and beings—
that is July's gift to us.

The Goddess of the Oven

There are quite a number of goddesses linked to the oven,
starting with Fornax, the Roman goddess of the hearth,
who is also linked to bread making and is particularly
fond of gifts of bread, cakes, and fruit. There is also Kamui
Fuchi, a Japanese hearth goddess who actually lives in the
oven and is credited with keeping us in touch with our
ancestral spirits; give her offerings of cooked rice and beer.
Then there is the Lithuanian hearth goddess Gabija; like
Fornax, she is also linked with the baking of bread and can
be honored by placing a small dish of salt or fresh water
near the stove.

There is one thing all these oven goddesses have in
common: they dislike dirty, untidy stoves (or kitchens in
general) and will withhold their blessings if they find the
oven to be in a mess! While I don't think cleaning the oven
would ever be at the top of anyone's list of favorite activi-

ties, this might be an incentive to keep your oven sparkling fresh.

In the warmth of July, we are probably going to be using the oven a lot less, so it's a good time to get it really clean. Try this simple cleaner: mix ½ cup baking soda with a little white vinegar to form a paste. Using gloves, apply this paste to the greasy, sticky parts of your oven and leave it there for at least half an hour. Then rinse off with lots of clean hot water: no noxious chemicals, and you can do this as often as needed. You can also add a few drops of lemon or lavender oil to the paste.

In Chinese feng shui, the oven is seen as the contemporary hearth, the source of heat and nourishment for the entire household and the bringer of abundance and good fortune. For this reason, it's considered unlucky to have clutter around the stove; also, don't leave empty pots on the stove, and if you have any burners that aren't working, get them fixed.

When you have finished cleaning your stove, sprinkle it lightly with a little salt water and say the following:

> *My kitchen is the heart of my home, and my*
> *stove is its hearth and its heart. May all the*
> *meals I make on this stove bring joy and*
> *nourishment on every level. May the goddesses*
> *bless my stove this day and always. And so it is.*

The Rainbow Kitchen

Color has a significant impact on us daily—on physical, spiritual, and emotional levels—and it's in the kitchen, in particular, that we can truly tap into the power of color! The foods we grow, buy, prepare, and cook all have their colors and can be stepping-stones to deeper truths and magic.

The foods listed below are all fruits and vegetables; obviously there are also many other foods to be found in these color families.

BLUE: the color of peace and spirituality, a color for creating inner calm and rest. There are a few naturally blue foods, such as blue corn, blueberries, and blue potatoes, but you can also use blue glassware or china as a lovely way of introducing blue into your meals. Use simple blue and white table linens or arrange a vase of little blue flowers on your kitchen table—choose flowers like baby blue eyes or forget-me-nots.

GREEN: probably one of the most significant and abundant colors we have, it's a symbol of earth and her many gifts to us—the gifts of growth, grounding, healing, peace, and replenishment.

Just a few of the greens we have to choose from: spinach, cabbage, green peppers, avocados, limes, lettuce, sprouts, peas and beans, zucchini (courgette), celery, green apples and grapes, brussels sprouts, and, of course, herbs!

ORANGE: another joyful color, orange creates a sense of confidence and enthusiasm; it brings people together in an expansive and connected way. Carrots, oranges, pumpkins, sweet potatoes, melons, nectarines, peaches, and apricots are all variations on the orange theme.

PURPLE: the magical color of intuition, psychic powers, and insight. To deepen and expand your natural wisdom and clairvoyance, use purple foods in your cooking such as plums, purple cabbage, figs, and eggplant.

RED: the color of passion, joy, and energy. If you are feeling low, anxious, and weak, red will give you a boost of both courage and new life. Red foods are abundant: tomatoes, red chilis, beets, red apples, red potatoes, watermelon, red onion, cherries, strawberries, raspberries ...

WHITE: this color's powerful and insightful energy is a divine source of healing and new awareness. White foods include onion, garlic, cauliflower, white potatoes, and parsnips.

YELLOW: bright and clear yellow is linked to sun energies and communication. Yellow helps us stay focused, clear, and joyful. Yellow foods include lemons, grapefruit, sweet corn, bananas, yellow peppers, summer squash, and pineapple.

Kitchen Pleasures

- Hydration is very important on these hot summer days, so keeping a few jugs of chilled herb and fruit waters around ensures that people will keep themselves healthy. Fill a large glass jug with spring water (still or sparkling) and add the chopped or sliced herbs and fruits of your choice. Some ideas for herbs and spices: mint, rosemary (just a little), lemon balm, geranium, ginger, basil. Fruits: strawberries, all citrus fruits, thinly sliced melon (or watermelon, pips removed), grapes, cucumber, mango. Keep the flavored water in the refrigerator and use within a day.

- Serenity Spell—for a calm and uplifting feeling in your kitchen, burn a small yellow candle that you have anointed with a few drops of bergamot, saffron, or neroli essential oil, and place a few small citrine crystals in front of the candle. Use this whenever the hot summer days seem to be leading to bad tempers and irritability.

- Use the magic of flowers and herbs to create scented sugars. Try adding rose petals, geranium leaves, lemon balm, jasmine flowers, lavender, or mint to a jar of sugar and leave it for a week or two, stirring occasionally. These sugars make wonderful additions to summer drinks and cocktails and can also be sprinkled on cookies or cakes.

- Cook and eat outside in the warmth of the sun whenever possible to breathe in the magic of this bountiful season. Make summer memories and record them in your kitchen journal, too.

RECIPES

Red Pepper, Olive, and Anchovy Compote

SERVES 6–8 AS A STARTER OR SIDE DISH

This utterly addictive summer recipe from France is wonderful for a lazy Sunday meal served with lots of fresh bread and some good cheese. And in this instance please don't leave out the anchovies, even if they are not your favorite thing—they really add a delicious taste dimension to this dish. Olives are, of course, a very ancient fruit with all kinds of traditional and spiritual powers, and red peppers are, like other members of the chili family, linked with creative energy and the breaking of bad spells or karma.

4 large red peppers
½ cup olive oil
4 ounces black olives, without stones
4 garlic cloves, crushed
A handful of fresh thyme, chopped
10 anchovies, drained
2 tablespoons fresh basil leaves
Black pepper

Place the red peppers on a baking sheet and broil until the skin of the peppers is starting to blacken. Remove, cool, and then skin the peppers. Slice thinly, removing the seeds.

Warm the olive oil in a large frying pan, then stir in the peppers, olives, and garlic, and cook gently for 10 minutes. Add the thyme and anchovies and continue to cook until the anchovies have dissolved into the sauce. Remove from the heat, and sprinkle with roughly torn basil leaves and black pepper to taste. Cool to room temperature and serve immediately.

Jellied Chicken and Ham Salad

SERVES 6–8

One of the most magical things about food and the recipes we prepare is the tangible connection they can bring between old and new, past and present, what is gone and yet still remains. For me, this simple jellied chicken recipe—my mom called it Chicken in Aspic—is one of those recipes. It reminds me of happy summer days eating out in the garden and playing with my cousins in the pool, but most of all, it reminds me of my uncle Frank, the most warm-hearted and gentle man I ever knew, taken away far, far too soon. He loved my mom's (his sister) chicken salad and begged her to make it every time they came visiting. I can picture him now, smiling as he spooned up a very

generous helping onto his plate! A kitchen is never just a kitchen—it's a place where memories are not only created but also stored and treasured.

If you don't want the hassle of cooking a chicken from scratch, you can use shredded cooked chicken and good-quality chicken broth instead.

> **1 medium chicken**
> **1 onion, chopped**
> **1 carrot, sliced**
> **A handful of fresh parsley**
> **Salt and pepper to taste**
> **½ cup dry white wine**
> **Juice of 1 lemon**
> **1 cup chopped ham (optional)**
> **1½ tablespoons gelatin**
> **¼ cup cold water**

Place the chicken in a large, deep saucepan and sprinkle with the onion, carrot, parsley, salt, pepper, white wine, and lemon juice. Add enough water to cover the chicken and simmer gently for 1½ hours or until chicken is soft and cooked through. (Skim off any white scum that rises to the top of the pot.) Remove the chicken and strain the stock, reserving the liquid. Remove skin and bones and chop or shred the chicken. (You will need about 3 cups of chicken for this recipe.)

Place the chicken in a suitable mold or bowl and mix in the ham (if using). Dissolve the gelatin in the cold water, then gently warm 2 cups of the stock and mix with the gelatin mixture until the gelatin is completely dissolved. Pour the stock mixture over the chicken, place in the fridge, and leave to set. Serve chilled with mayonnaise mixed with a little lemon juice/chopped lemon zest and a green salad.

Sunshine Potato Salad

SERVES 4–6

Is there anyone who doesn't like potato salad? To me, it always symbolizes the warm, bright days of summer—days spent outdoors, days of picnics, barbecues, and happy celebrations of every kind. Potatoes are such protective and grounding vegetables, and the dill (and dill pickles) in this recipe add to the nurturing qualities of this dish. You will note that this is a potato salad without mayonnaise, making it lighter and more refreshing to eat. You can add some cooked chopped bacon, sliced hard-cooked egg, or pitted (stoned) olives to make a more substantial salad.

> 2 pounds small waxy potatoes
> 1 small red onion, very finely chopped
> 6 small dill pickles, thinly sliced
> A small handful of fresh dill, snipped fine
> 2 tablespoons fresh parsley, chopped

¼ cup olive oil

¼ cup fresh lemon juice

1 small clove garlic, crushed

Salt and pepper to taste

Boil the potatoes (peeled or not, as you prefer) in a large pan of simmering water until just soft but not mushy. Drain, cool, and slice. Place potatoes in a serving bowl and stir in the onion, dill pickles, dill, and parsley. In a small bowl or cup, whisk together the olive oil, lemon juice, garlic, salt, and pepper to make a dressing. Pour over the potatoes, toss well, and then chill until serving.

Chocolate Ice Cream with Caramel Sauce

MAKES 1 QUART ICE CREAM & 1½ CUPS SAUCE

My mother made this simple ice cream all the time when I was growing up; it was part of her summer kitchen routine. And it really is easy to make—one doesn't need an ice cream maker or even have to beat the mixture once the ice cream is in the freezer. Ice cream has all the magic and nurturing qualities linked with dairy products, as well as being imbued with the feminine powers and spirituality of the moon. This can be adapted into different flavored ice creams by replacing the cocoa mixture with strong coffee, lemon or orange juice, passionfruit or strawberry pulp... use your imagination!

½ cup cocoa powder

½ cup hot water

1 teaspoon vanilla extract

1 large can sweetened condensed milk

2 cups heavy cream

½ teaspoon salt

Mix the cocoa and hot water together in a small bowl to form a smooth paste, then stir in the vanilla extract. Allow to cool, then add the condensed milk and mix together until smooth.

In another large bowl, beat the cream until fairly stiff. Add the salt and gently fold the cocoa mixture into the cream, ensuring it is well incorporated. Pour into a suitable container and place in the freezer until firm. Remove from the freezer about 10 minutes before serving.

Caramel Sauce

In a heavy-bottomed saucepan, melt ½ stick butter with ½ cup sugar and ½ cup water and stir until the sugar is completely dissolved. Add 1 cup heavy cream and cook over low heat, stirring frequently, until the mixture is thick and smooth. Remove from the heat, add ½ teaspoon vanilla extract, and cool the sauce before pouring it into a jar and storing it in the refrigerator.

Lemon and Passionfruit Pavlova

SERVES 6

Light and bursting with bright citrus and fruit flavors, this makes an enchanted finale to any summer meal. Eggs and lemon offer all kinds of protective and magical qualities, and as for the humble little passionfruit—well, it's known for bringing peace, love, and good karma to any situation. Make this dessert on the day you plan to serve it, if possible, as meringue is always at its crisp and ethereal best when freshly baked.

Preheat oven to 275°F. Line a large baking sheet with parchment (baking) paper.

> 2 egg whites
> ¼ teaspoon cream of tartar
> ½ cup superfine sugar
> 1 large can sweetened condensed milk
> ½ cup fresh lemon juice
> Zest of 1 large lemon
> 1 cup passionfruit pulp
> 2 cups heavy cream

Place the egg whites in a very clean, dry bowl together with the cream of tartar and beat until soft peaks form. Add the sugar gradually and continue beating to form a stiff meringue. Spread the mixture to form a circle (approximately 9–10 inches in diameter) on the prepared baking

sheet, making it a little higher at the sides. Bake 70 to 80 minutes or until the meringue is a very light gold and firm. Cool.

To make the filling, place the condensed milk in a bowl and stir in the lemon juice, zest, and ¼ cup of the passionfruit pulp. Mix well. In another small glass bowl, beat the cream till soft peaks form, then fold this into the condensed milk mixture gently and thoroughly. Just before serving, spread the mixture in the prepared meringue shell and garnish with the reserved passionfruit pulp.

PANTRY

Tomato Passion Chutney

MAKES ABOUT 3 CUPS

No summer kitchen should ever be without tomatoes—lots of them, from the tiny little round ones to the huge slicing tomatoes and all the shapes and colors in between. They are a vital part of any cook's pantry. What would Italian cooking be, for example, without the humble tomato? Tomatoes, which are technically a fruit, also carry all sorts of enchanted energy and were originally known as "love apples" because of their reputation for inciting both love and passion.

This summer recipe, which you can enjoy eating well into fall and winter, is a spicy tomato chutney that a friend started calling "Tomato Passion"—and for obvious reasons; it really is quite addictive. Share it with someone you love! This sauce is delicious served with meat, barbecue, curries, and other spicy dishes.

½ cup vegetable oil

2 tablespoons grated fresh ginger

2 garlic cloves, crushed

3 or 4 chilies, seeded and chopped

2 tablespoons mustard seeds

2 teaspoons turmeric

2 tablespoons ground cumin

1 teaspoon cayenne pepper

2 pounds ripe tomatoes, peeled
   and coarsely chopped

1 cup apple cider vinegar

½ cup brown sugar

Salt to taste

Heat the oil in a very large pan, then gently fry the ginger, garlic, and chilies for a few minutes. Stir in the mustard seeds, turmeric, cumin, and cayenne pepper, and continue frying for 5 minutes. Add the tomatoes to the mixture together with the vinegar, brown sugar, and salt. Simmer on low heat for at least an hour, stirring from time to time, until the mixture begins to thicken and the oil rises to the surface. Remove from the heat, cool briefly, then spoon into sterilized glass jars and seal. Store in the refrigerator once open.

Lemon Verbena and Geranium Syrup

MAKES ABOUT 2½ CUPS

This herbal syrup positively sings of summer with its fresh and delicate taste, and it incorporates two of my most favorite herbs. If you don't have lemon verbena available, you can also use lemon balm leaves—or, if all else fails, simply add the juice and zest of a fresh lemon to the infusion. I like to use rose geranium leaves for this syrup, but the mint or peppermint ones also work—they just create a slightly sharper and more tangy syrup.

You can omit the alcohol if you prefer, but it does ensure the syrup has a more lasting quality. Either way, use a few spoonfuls of this syrup in sparkling water, cocktails, iced tea, and fruit punches for a green burst of flavor.

> 1 large handful lemon verbena leaves
> 1 large handful rose geranium leaves
> 2 cups boiling water
> 2 cups sugar
> ½ cup raw honey
> ¾ cup vodka (optional)

Roughly tear the lemon verbena and rose geranium leaves and place in a large glass bowl or jug. Pour the boiling water over the leaves and allow the herbs to infuse for at least an hour. Then strain the liquid very well and place in a saucepan with the sugar. Simmer gently until the sugar has dissolved, then stir in the honey and mix well. Remove from the heat and add the vodka (if using). Allow the syrup to cool, then pour it into small, sterilized glass bottles and store in the fridge.

In this moment, there is infinite possibility.

Victoria Moran

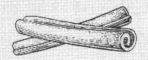

AUGUST

Changes and Shifting Patterns

*A*t the end of summer, light changes and patterns shift as the earth prepares to yield her summer harvest of bounty. It's a time for us to plan our own harvest as we move towards the fall and enjoy the gifts we have been given at this time.

Lammas (Lughnasadh) comes at the beginning of August, the first of the traditional harvest festivals honoring the grains that nourish us and the farmers that have grown them over the centuries. We often talk about the "bread of life"; bread is an important symbol and sacrament in both the Christian and Judaic traditions. Nowadays many of us are starting to bake our own bread again and finding both blessing and privilege in this ancient art, but even if regular breadmaking is not on the cards, give it a try at this particular season of harvest and plenty. Nothing says magic in a kitchen quite like a loaf of bread fresh from the oven—a miracle of transformation from a soft lump of wet dough to a golden and aromatic loaf!

Nothing is said to be quite as grounding or peaceful as the art of making bread. While our bread dough rises, or once it is in the oven, we can sit quietly in our comfortable chair and think about our lives, which are not that dissimilar to bread. We grow and develop and are shaped by forces both within and beyond ourselves. Sometimes these forces knead us into shapes we did not expect or want, but we still rise. We still emerge. We are still life, just like the bread we bake.

In this month we honor and celebrate the Roman goddess of the harvest, Ceres (and her Greek counterpart, Demeter). They represent all that is nurturing and fruitful on this earth—and, by definition, all the abundance and potential harvest we also possess as human beings—so perhaps it's no coincidence that Ceres is also a goddess of fertility and motherhood. In August when we bake or eat breads (and other grain dishes), we are honoring both the earth and our own bodies and spirits. And please always remember never to waste bread—the goddesses take a very dim

view of that. If bread has gone stale, it can be crumbled and frozen for later use in recipes like stuffings or fried chicken.

Once, many years ago, I found a blessing for bread in a very old cookbook. I scribbled it down on a piece of note paper but now have no recollection of the book it came from. It is beautifully appropriate for the harvest time, for bread, and for blessing our own lives.

Bless the seed. Bless the soil. Bless the grower. Bless the light and rain. Bless the harvest. We are all blessed, and we are all harvest. We can grow in the light. We can be shaped and changed by the fire. We can be made new and we can be nourishment. We are both blessing and bread.

Finding the Wabi-Sabi Moment in the Kitchen

I am writing this book in early 2021, after a year that has shaken and shifted our world and lives like no other. Things have changed, sometimes irrevocably, sometimes painfully, and sometimes for the better, even though that might be hard to see for those who have lost loved ones, work, financial security, and more.

Using the theme of shifting patterns for this month of August, we can also learn to see that these changing times

and seasons will ultimately bring us to a stronger and more beautiful whole. We are learning to look beyond the need for perfection and simply find joy and comfort in what is—because perfection is neither necessary nor helpful, not that it ever has been. I say this as a recovering perfectionist, particularly when it comes to food and cooking. I have been known to toss out an entire cake because it didn't look right!

Now, here, in our kitchens—wherever and whatever they may be—we can learn to be in the moment, which is perfect in its own imperfect way. The kitchen is a reflection of ourselves and of the things we love and hold dear, the things we want to create and cherish. Wabi sabi is the traditional Japanese way of seeing beauty in the moment, imperfect or flawed as it may be; it's a concept that truly can help us live in the here and now without stress or regret, and I recommend it highly. I also recommend a lovely and insightful little book by Beth Kempton simply titled *Wabi Sabi: Japanese Wisdom for a Perfectly Imperfect Life*. A friend gave me this book as a gift a few years ago, and it has made a huge difference in the way I choose to see and live my life every day.

As I sit in my kitchen drinking my morning cappuccino, I look at the beautiful feathers clustered in an old copper jug—feathers gifted to me by the birds who are my daily

sweet-voiced companions. I look at the dachshund mug that my mother gave me a few years ago, after the death of my little dog after seventeen years of companionship. That mug has been dropped and repaired quite a few times now and is no longer fit to be used for hot drinks, but I keep it on my shelf because it reminds me of love and connection and precisely because it isn't perfect. It doesn't have to be. Neither do we; we are all shifting, changing with the years and the seasons, with things that happen, sometimes without our control or understanding. But the gift of real enchantment doesn't require understanding; it only requires that we be open to it, notice it, and invite it in.

If you are struggling with changes and shifts in your own life and the world around you, here is a simple and gentle ritual I often find helpful. It's best to do this alone, when your kitchen is quiet and still; I prefer either early morning or late evening. Find something you love—something old and precious (to you)—and place it on your table. Light a candle—again, simply choose a color you particularly enjoy. I like to add a few drops of rosemary oil (for memory) and lemon oil (for clarity) to the candle.

Ground yourself, then light the candle and sit quietly for a few moments. I find this to be quite an emotive ritual, which can bring up strong feelings and tears—tissues are

allowed! Take time with this ritual; the candle can be left burning for a while and later extinguished carefully.

Say or read the following:

> *I am here, in this moment. It's what I have, and this is my life, the life I am living now. It is what it is. And I can choose to find the joy and the beauty in this moment as it is. I am here in my kitchen, a safe place. I have learned that nothing is perfect or ever will be. But I already have all I need for my life, and I am blessed by this. I am blessed by our earth, by the seasons, by everything I see and experience today. I choose to honor myself and my life as perfectly imperfect. And so it is.*

I also often explore this whole concept of wabi sabi when writing in my kitchen journal—I remind myself that, just like everything else, my cooking does not have to be perfect! I am going to make mistakes and end up with food that is just a little off center, and that is okay. It's part of my growing and learning. So, next time a recipe really doesn't work out, write about it in your journal—maybe there are lessons to be learned there, but we can still enjoy what we created here and now.

Fruitful Blessings

Fruits are probably often one of the things we take for granted, grabbing a banana for a quick snack as we are heading out the door or tucking an apple in our child's backpack. They possess such ancient and magical qualities that we should enjoy and use them as often as possible— after all, apples were one of the first fruits ever recorded, although history now relates that it might have been a fig or a quince that Eve actually plucked in the mystical garden of Eden.

APPLE: healing, abundance, and prosperity

APRICOT: reputedly an aphrodisiac, with lots of love and sexual energies.

AVOCADO: beauty, joy, and fertility

BANANA: sacred to the goddess Venus and ideal for fertility and protection purposes.

BLACKBERRY: sacred to the faeries, these little berries help boost both creativity and prosperity.

BLUEBERRY: sacred to the goddess Brigid, blueberries give us psychic protection against negative and potentially harmful forces.

CHERRY: a magical tree with beautiful blossoms in the spring; use the fruit and stones for divination and to create magical new beginnings.

FIG: this small fruit was sacred in ancient Greece and was used for meditation, consecration, and fertility rites.

GRAPE: well, aside from wine, grapes are another fruit sacred in both ancient Greece and Rome; they have a lot of spiritual energy and are linked to, and ruled by, the moon.

LEMON: an absolute must in any kitchen, lemons are not only delicious in so many recipes, both sweet and savory, but they pack a powerful range of magical qualities, from protection to purification to love and friendship.

LIME: shares many of lemon's qualities, although limes are generally quite a bit more tart; use them to block dark or malevolent forces.

MANGO: sacred to the Buddha, mango is a strongly spiritual fruit; also used to increase love and fertility.

MELONS: ruled by the moon and the element of water, melons are helpful for all kinds of cleansing and healing purposes.

ORANGE: a happy and positive fruit of the sun, oranges are bringers of luck, good fortune, happiness, and creative energy.

PASSIONFRUIT: although you would imagine the name says it all, this little fruit is also helpful if you need a sense of calm, peace, and clarity in your life.

PEACH: another magical tree also linked to Venus, peach is a sign of spring blessings, fertility, love, and longevity.

PEAR: this fruit shares many of the qualities of peaches and also has lots of passionate energies, so serve pears in salads and desserts if you want to spice up your love connections.

PINEAPPLE: there are lots of masculine energies in this fruit, and it's also linked with prosperity, good luck, and healing on both physical and emotional levels.

PLUM: in ancient China, these little fruits were reputed to be a symbol of wisdom, longevity, and rebirth.

POMEGRANATE: a truly magical fruit linked to Persephone and Ceres/Demeter and often used

at Samhain for magical workings involving death, the afterlife, and the granting of wishes.

Raspberry: another feminine fruit ruled by Venus, raspberry has lots of love and passion energy.

Strawberry: sacred to Freya, Frigg, and Aphrodite, strawberry is a fruit of love and fertility; the leaves are also magical when used in spells for luck, success, and prosperity.

Tomato: folk names like love apple and wolf peach indicate tomato's energies of love, passion, and protection.

Enchanted Culinary Oils

Oils are a specially magical part of any kitchen witch's culinary repertoire. This is just a brief listing of some of the oils we are most likely to have around, and although some of these oils can be used for more than just cooking (for example, in the making of natural skincare and beauty products), in this instance I am focusing on their kitchen use. Oils are so versatile in that they can be flavored in lots of different ways with the judicious addition of herbs and spices.

Please note that in order to keep your oils fresh and delicious, they should always be stored in a cool, dark place,

away from heat sources, and preferably in dark glass bottles with tight caps. Use oils within six months to a year, and discard any oils that have become cloudy or smell rancid.

ALMOND OIL: a highly magical oil that is not generally used for cooking, although a little can be added to cold or uncooked dishes. Almonds carry the magic qualities of protection, psychic power, and divination, and can bring you prosperity and good fortune.

AVOCADO OIL: a delicately flavored oil, often very pale green in color, this oil is wonderful in salad dressings and other uncooked dishes but is not generally suitable for frying. It's fairly expensive so should be used where its flavor really shines through. Like the avocado itself, the oil is linked with beauty, joy, and fertility.

CANOLA OIL: one of the most inexpensive and widely used oils, it's suitable for all kinds of cooking and baking. It is extremely low in saturated fat, making it a healthy choice, too.

COCONUT OIL: this oil has become very popular in recent years, and it is particularly useful in vegetarian and vegan baking and cooking. It does give a slightly nutty flavor to dishes but can also

be purchased in a deodorized or unflavored form. Use coconut oil where you would use sunflower oil, but note that it tends to solidify if left in a cold place. Coconuts are sacred to the Greek goddess Athena and have a strong connection to the moon and feminine energy in general. It's a cleansing and protective oil that is linked to consecration of all kinds.

Corn Oil: another good all-purpose cooking oil that is very high in polyunsaturated fat, this oil is linked to many gods and goddesses, among them Dionysus, Ceres, Isis, and Adonis. This oil has the energies of abundance, fertility, and prosperity.

Grapeseed Oil: this light oil, which is a byproduct of wine production, is one of my favorites— perhaps not surprisingly, it's linked to the god of wine, Bacchus, among others. It's not really suitable for cooking with heat but adds a lovely flavor to salad dressings and the like. Grapes are sacred to the moon and have lots of feminine energy; they are also symbolic of prosperity, abundance, and a good harvest.

Olive Oil: probably one of the most popular oils, with many different uses. Olive oils are available

in extra-virgin (the purest and generally more expensive option), first-pressed, and light forms. Blended olive oils, usually mixed with canola or sunflower oils, are also available, but I don't generally recommend those. Light olive oil is suitable for baking recipes that call for the use of oil; the stronger olive oils are also sometimes used for baking bread. Olive oil is not suitable for deep frying as it has a fairly low heat point; it's great for stir-fries and other shallow frying, though, and is also wonderful in salad dressings and uncooked sauces. Keep it on a cool, dark shelf in your pantry or kitchen and it will last for at least a year. Olive oil is sacred to the Greek gods Apollo, Athena, Poseidon, and Minerva, and, like olives themselves, it is full of magical properties, including spirituality, peace, healing, luck, and success.

PEANUT OIL: of course peanuts are not actually nuts at all but members of the legume family. The oil derived from peanuts is popular in Eastern cooking and because it has a high heat point, it can be used for deep frying. Peanut oil is a powerful energy-boosting oil with a lot of strong, masculine powers.

Sesame Oil: mostly used in Asian cooking and available in both light and dark forms; only the lighter form of sesame oil is suitable for deep frying. It is often fairly expensive, so I tend to use it predominantly in salad dressings and stir-fries. It's traditionally linked with both the goddess Hecate and the Hindu god Ganesh, and it holds the energies of protection and prosperity for the household.

Sunflower Oil: probably one of the most widely used and affordable of the culinary oils, it can be used for just about any cooking purpose, including deep frying, as it is odorless and has a high smoke point. I also like its association with the bright warmth and wisdom of sunflowers!

Kitchen Pleasures

- Bake an apple cake, pie, or crisp in honor of Pomona, the rosy-cheeked Roman goddess and protector of orchards, whose feast day was traditionally celebrated in August.

- Do you have a glut of peppers? Grill them, then peel, seed, and slice them and place in sterilized jars; cover with olive oil and store in a cool, dark place. Use in salads, stir-fries, and other recipes for a bright burst of summer all year round.

- Make herbal pestos and sauces using the last of the fresh summer herbs; they can be stored or frozen for months. Please note that the pesto recipe on page 79 can be adapted to suit all kinds of different herbs.

- Olives are little magical gifts from Minerva, the Greek goddess of wisdom. The olive tree gives shelter, food, and oil; use its healing gifts freely in both your cooking and kitchen.

RECIPES

Carrot, Apple, and Scallion Soup

SERVES 4

This dairy-free soup can be served either warm or chilled in the dog days of August. Apples are such a magical fruit, bringing blessings for a happy home, and carrots have wonderful protective qualities. You can use either red or green apples, but I prefer red as they add a little more sweetness. For pure enchantment, serve as a light meal with salad and sliced homemade bread in the early evening twilight.

> 2 tablespoons vegetable oil
> 1 onion, finely chopped
> 4 carrots, peeled and sliced
> A few celery stalks, sliced
> 2 tablespoons crushed ginger
> 2 apples, peeled and sliced
> 2 potatoes, peeled and chopped
> A handful of chopped scallions
> Parsley or mint for garnish

Warm the oil in a large saucepan, then fry the onion, carrots, celery, and ginger until the onions are soft and golden. Add the apples, potatoes, and scallions; cover with 2–3 cups water and simmer until the vegetables are tender, adding more water if necessary. Remove from the heat and puree with a stick blender or in a food processor. This soup can be served warm (not hot)—or, preferably, chilled in small bowls and topped with chopped parsley or mint.

Chicken, Tomato, and Pasta Bake

SERVES 4–6

I love cooking, but sometimes I have neither the inclination nor the time to spend all day in the kitchen! This is where one-pot dishes are the kitchen witch's solution to time and energy constraints. This particular recipe, inspired by Greek and Cypriot dishes, is a grounding and colorful meal-in-one—all it needs is a big green salad alongside, and maybe a glass of crisp white wine. I like to use salty Halloumi cheese, but if you can't get it, use well-drained feta instead.

> **6–8 chicken thighs/breasts, skin on**
> **2 red onions, sliced**
> **1 clove garlic, crushed**
> **2 tablespoons olive oil**
> **¼ cup fresh lemon juice**
> **½ cup dry white wine**

1 tablespoon honey

½ teaspoon salt

½ pound small pasta shells/macaroni

2–3 ripe tomatoes, sliced

3 ounces Halloumi cheese, crumbled

A few sprigs of fresh oregano

Preheat oven to 350°F.

Arrange the chicken pieces in a greased baking dish and sprinkle the red onions and garlic over the top. Combine the olive oil, lemon juice, wine, and honey, pour over the chicken, and roast uncovered for 1 hour or until the chicken pieces are cooked through and skin is golden brown.

Fill a large saucepan with water, add the salt, and then boil the pasta until al dente—it should not be overcooked and mushy. Drain very well and spread the pasta in the bottom of a large oven dish. Arrange the chicken and onions on top of the pasta, reserving the cooking juices from the chicken. Add enough water to the chicken cooking liquid to bring it up to 1 cup, then pour evenly over the chicken. Tuck the sliced tomatoes around the chicken pieces, then sprinkle the Halloumi cheese and oregano on top. Bake in the oven for 15 to 20 minutes or until the cheese has melted and the tomatoes have softened. Serve warm.

Cucumber-Mint Salad

This is an absolutely refreshing and magical salad for the last days of summer. Cucumber is packed with feminine and moon energy, so it is ideal for supporting emotional growth and well-being; mint, too, is a protective and calming herb widely used in magical healing of all kinds.

> 4 large cucumbers
>
> ½ teaspoon salt
>
> 1 clove of garlic, crushed
>
> 2 tablespoons white wine vinegar
>
> 1 cup plain or Greek yogurt
>
> 1 teaspoon cumin seeds
>
> 2 tablespoons olive oil
>
> 3 tablespoons fresh mint, chopped

Peel the cucumbers and slice them thinly. Place in a bowl and sprinkle with the salt, crushed garlic, and vinegar. Place in the fridge for 30 minutes, then drain, reserving the liquid. In a serving bowl, stir together the yogurt and reserved cucumber liquid, cumin seeds, and olive oil. Add the drained cucumber slices and mix well. Sprinkle with finely chopped mint and serve as soon as possible.

Late Summer Crisp

SERVES 6

This simple and cozy dessert is packed with bright flavors and feminine energies from both the raspberries and peaches. Raspberries are a fruit of love, linked to the goddesses Venus, Aphrodite, Isis, and Hecate. Serve this to someone you love to ensure their devotion … or, at the very least, to spark their interest. You can use canned peaches if you can't get fresh ones, and nectarines also work well.

Preheat oven to 400°F. Grease a deep 9-inch pie plate.

4 or 5 ripe peaches, peeled and cut into thick slices
¾ pound fresh raspberries
1½ cups flour
¼ cup sugar
1 teaspoon vanilla extract
1¼ sticks butter, chilled
¼ cup shredded coconut
2 tablespoons brown sugar

Mix peach slices with raspberries and arrange in the bottom of the pie plate. In a bowl, combine the flour, sugar, and vanilla extract, then rub in the chilled butter with your fingers until the mixture looks like coarse breadcrumbs. Stir in the coconut and then sprinkle the flour mixture liberally all over the fruit in the pie plate, covering it as much as possible. Sprinkle with the brown sugar. Bake the crisp

197

for 30 to 35 minutes or until the fruit is soft and the topping golden brown. Serve warm, preferably with a scoop of vanilla ice cream.

Herb Pull-Apart Bread

MAKES 4–6 SIDE SERVINGS

This is something rather special, a beautiful centerpiece for a harvest table when served with soup, salad, or cheese. My mom used to make it many years ago, but only recently, when I started making it again, did I remember how special it—and she—was. That's the beauty of kitchen magic—it takes you on many wonderful journeys! Use any fresh herbs you like; I prefer a combination of finely chopped oregano and parsley, which goes well with the cheese.

> 1 cup whole milk
>
> 2 tablespoons butter
>
> 1 tablespoon sugar
>
> ½ teaspoon salt
>
> 2¼ teaspoons dried yeast
>
> 2 tablespoons water
>
> 1 egg
>
> 2½–3 cups bread flour
>
> 2 tablespoons chopped herbs
>
> ¼ cup grated Parmesan

In a small saucepan, gently warm the milk, butter, sugar, and salt until the butter has melted. Remove from the heat and cool slightly. In a large bowl, mix the dried yeast and water to form a paste, then stir in the milk mixture and the egg. Gradually add the flour to form a soft but not sticky dough; lastly knead in the herbs and cheese, then turn out onto a floured surface and knead for 5 minutes. Shape the dough into a ball and place in a bowl; cover and leave in a warm place to rise until doubled in bulk—about an hour.

Preheat the oven to 425°F. Grease a round or square 8-inch baking pan with melted butter.

Punch the risen dough down, then shape it into 12–16 small balls and arrange snugly into the baking pan. Cover and allow to rise again. Bake 25 to 30 minutes or until risen and golden brown. Cool briefly on a wire rack, then turn out and serve warm. This bread can also be sprinkled with a little crushed garlic or more fresh herbs before serving.

PANTRY

Salsa di Pomodoro

MAKES ABOUT 4 CUPS

Tomatoes were regarded with some suspicion in the Middle Ages; they were believed to promote lust and wild passion, probably because of their rich and vibrant color. Now they are an indispensable part of any enchanted kitchen, linked as they are to love and passion while also offering psychic and physical protection. Planting tomatoes in your garden helps to dispel unwanted negative energies. Above all, they should be used freely and with joy when they are in season—ripe, red, overflowing with juicy abundance ...

My Italian father loved this simple sauce over pasta or vegetables or just eaten by the spoonful. It's very easy to make and can be stored in the fridge for a couple of weeks. Both the chili and wine are optional; if you choose not to use the wine, simply add more water. And I am not a fan of tomato skins, so I prefer to peel the tomatoes before cooking them; however, this is a matter of personal preference.

3 tablespoons olive oil

1 large onion, peeled and chopped fine

4 garlic cloves, peeled and crushed

1 green chili, chopped finely

2½ pounds ripe tomatoes

A handful of fresh basil leaves

½ cup dry white wine

½ cup water

Salt and pepper to taste

½ teaspoon sugar or to taste

Heat the olive oil in a large, deep saucepan, and fry the onion, garlic, and chili for a few minutes or until softened and golden. Chop the tomatoes (peeled or not, see above) and the basil leaves, and add to the saucepan together with the wine and water. Add salt, pepper, and sugar to taste.

Cover and simmer gently for 15 to 20 minutes or until the sauce starts to thicken and smell wonderful, then remove the lid and continue simmering for another 10 to 15 minutes. The sauce should be fairly thick and rich red in color. Remove from the heat and allow to cool before spooning into sterilized glass jars. You can use a blender or food processor if you prefer a very smooth sauce, but I like it to remain a little chunky. Store in the fridge for up to 2 weeks.

Spiced Ghee

Ghee is a form of clarified butter traditional in both Indian and Ayurvedic cooking. As a pure butter, with the milk solids removed, it's rich in vitamins and easily digested. I love this particular ghee recipe as its subtle spice flavor makes it ideal for adding to lots of dishes, from rice to curries to stir-fries. Of course, you can add your own herb and spice combinations, too—and remember, butter is a favorite of the faeries!

To make the butter, gently warm 2 cups unsalted butter in a deep pan; after a while, a white, foamy layer will start to form on top. Skim off this foam and continue gently heating the melted butter until the foam solids sink to the bottom, leaving a clear golden liquid on top.

Remove from the heat and stir in the following:

1 onion, chopped

3 crushed garlic cloves

A small piece of fresh ginger

2 cloves

2 coriander seeds

A pinch each of ground nutmeg and cumin

Stand for 15 minutes until the flavors have infused into the butter, then strain the mixture carefully through a piece of muslin or cheesecloth; you might have to do this more than once. Pour the cooled ghee into a large sterilized glass jar and allow to cool completely before sealing. It will keep well for a couple of months stored on a cool shelf that is not in direct sun or in contact with heat sources.

In seed time learn,
in harvest teach,
in winter enjoy...

William Blake

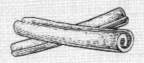

SEPTEMBER

Gifts of the Harvest

September 20–23 marks the autumnal equinox, known as Mabon in the traditional wheel of the year: the time when day and night are of equal length before the darkness lengthens and the earth slips down towards the wintertime. It's a liminal season, one in which we stand between the light and the dark, and it represents both the richness of the harvest and the need to let go in many aspects of life, both physical and spiritual. As such, it's a powerful time of the year that is sacred to many different gods and goddesses such as Ceres and her daughter Persephone (this season also celebrates the bonds between mothers and daughters) and Freya, a Norse goddess of fertility, harvest, and female sexual power.

Originally Mabon was part of Celtic mythology and told the story of a young man's rescue from the forces of darkness and the underworld—of course, harvest festivals later became an important part of the Christian year. When I was a young girl, we would all attend church services for harvest home, and each of us had to bring a small basket filled with fruits, nuts, and other good things such as a loaf of bread or home-baked cookies. After the service was concluded, we all trooped up to the front of the church and left our baskets there, to be distributed later among various shelters or charitable organizations.

Perhaps this is reflective of how we are all connected, in so many ways, whatever path or form of belief we choose to follow. The earth nurtures and sustains all of us, and sharing is an important part of our individual and collective journeys, especially at this time on the planet when so many people are struggling with poverty and lack as never before.

But even more than the practical aspects, September offers us the opportunity to reflect on our own personal harvests for the year—what have we planted, what seeds

have taken hold, what has grown in our lives? What, too, do we need to let go of with grace and acceptance, in much the same way as the leaves drift softly down from the tree branches that sustained them through the summer?

There are a few kitchen rituals that seem particularly appropriate for this time of year. Firstly, bring apples into your kitchen. Red, ripe, shiny apples are truly magical fruit, and the apple tree is seen as one of the most enchanted of all, for it is the gateway between this world and the shining light that waits beyond in the Summerland, the Land of the Ever Young. Place an apple on your kitchen altar or arrange a row of apples on your windowsill. If you carve a small hole in the top of each apple just big enough to insert a tealight, it looks beautiful; when the lights are burning, they give a totally magical and otherworldly look to the apples. And when you are done with the apples, chop them up, skin and all, and leave them out for the birds to feast on.

In Inca legend, September 20 marked the birthday of the sun, and you can honor his coming, too, by bringing marigolds, oranges, sunflower seeds, and a handful of whole spices (cinnamon sticks, nutmeg, or star anise) into your kitchen decorations or adding them to the kitchen altar.

A Honey Blessing

Honey is a messenger from the gods and the spirit world symbolic of happiness, prosperity, and new blessings. You do need a beeswax candle for this, as well as some lavender for cleansing and a small dish of honey. Light the candle, then burn the herb and allow the smoke to gently drift around the candle and the dish of honey that you have placed next to the candle. You can also use a diffuser and suitable oils, if you prefer.

This is a lovely ritual to do with others, too, or with children; do this ritual as often as you like in the season of harvest, allowing the candle to burn for at least an hour.

I light this candle, symbol of the light, the light
that has sustained us through this year … the
light that brought the harvest to us. Earth has
shared her gifts with us, and we, in turn, have
grown and learned lessons from the seasons and
changes. It is well; it is as it should be. This life
on earth is a cycle, one we share—a harvest of
hope we can reap again and again. As I blow
out the candle, I remember that I too am both
light and darkness. This is a complete cycle,
and I am blessed to share in it. And so it is.

A Harvest Kitchen Journal

In our kitchen journals for this month, it is good to reflect on what we have to be grateful for—in our kitchens and in our lives. What foods have we shared, what memories have we created, what harvest of taste are we going to carry forward into the cold and dark winter months?

I like to write down some recipes that remind me just how much I have to be grateful for—the memory of collected tastes and meals given and shared over the years. This month is also linked to the bonds between mothers and daughters, so this is a good time to honor and celebrate these as well; as I've said before, my mother and I had a fairly volatile and often difficult relationship, but it was in the kitchen that we connected best. I choose to remember her in this way by using some of the recipes she passed down to me or by creating a dish that I know she loved. Even though she is no longer here on a physical plane to enjoy it, I believe she tastes my love and affection still.

If you have harvested some of your own herbs, fruits, or vegetables, choose or create some new recipes for using them. Write them in your journal as a sign of the growth and learning we have in each year and in every moment.

The Fire of Kali

Kali is a Hindu goddess, and I was not really familiar with her until I did a course on Indian cooking in London some years ago. Meena's kitchen was one of the most colorful and aromatic cooking spaces I had ever seen, full of spicy aromas and bright warmth. Just being in her kitchen was like a magic carpet ride to some exotic fairytale. She also had a number of little shrines in her kitchen with small clay figures, candles, and incense. One of them, a rather wild-looking woman adorned with skulls and with her tongue protruding, was not familiar to me. "That's Kali," Meena said when I asked. "The Hindu goddess of death and destruction."

She must have seen the look on my face because she went on to explain that Kali is also a powerfully protective goddess, helping us to burn away what no longer serves us and rise again from the ashes of past lives into new self-empowerment and growth. That, too, is a lesson we take from Mabon, so it seemed appropriate to include her in this chapter as the kitchen goddess. In actual fact, Kali Puja—the feast of Kali—is celebrated in India and elsewhere around the middle of November, close to Diwali.

Let us honor Kali and all those, seen and unseen, who help us let go of what is past and move towards new beginnings and horizons with open and joyful hearts. Plan a feast of bright and colorful Eastern foods, as hot and spicy as you like. Burn lots of Nag Champa incense, use your most colorful dishes and bowls, and spread a red or gold cloth over the kitchen table. The light is always there for us, even as the days grow shorter, for we carry it within ourselves; it is part of our birthright on this beautiful earth.

Kitchen Pleasures

- September 15 is celebrated as the birthday of the moon in China. Bake moon-shaped cakes and cookies or plan a feast including lunar foods such as eggs, lemons, fish, potatoes, coconuts, and mushrooms. If possible, eat them outside in the moonlight.

- On the festival of Durga (September 7), honor the Himalayan goddess of the earth by eating lots of seasonal fruit and vegetables. Try something new that you haven't tasted or cooked with before.

- Gather autumn leaves to decorate your kitchen. Pin them to a ribbon and create a colorful swag for your curtains or simply scatter a few bright leaves down the middle of your kitchen table.

- Bake corn bread or muffins for a fall picnic or breakfast; they echo the golden light and warmth of this time of year.

RECIPES

Mushroom Pâté

MAKES ABOUT 1½ CUPS, ENOUGH FOR 4–6
AS A SNACK OR APPETIZER

Mushrooms seem to be a particularly magical part of fall, making one think of misty mornings under a canopy of trees, falling leaves crackling underfoot, and the scent of woodsmoke in the air. They are linked to faery magic, too, which is not surprising given that they often seem to appear and disappear as if by some strange enchantment.

Mushrooms are linked to the moon and possess her dark and powerful energies, yet they are also powerfully grounding, too, given the way they emerge from the earth. Eat mushrooms for balance, courage, and mystical powers! This vegetarian pâté is both simple to prepare and delicious with breads and savory crackers. I usually cover it with a layer of melted butter since the color of the dish is not that appealing to the eye, but this is a matter of personal preference.

½ stick butter

1½ pounds brown or white mushrooms, sliced

1 small onion, finely chopped

1 clove garlic, crushed

1 tablespoon soy sauce

2 tablespoons brandy

1 tablespoon fresh thyme, chopped

½ teaspoon black pepper

½ cup sour cream

Extra butter & sprigs of thyme for garnish

Melt the butter in a large frying pan and fry the sliced mushrooms, onion, and garlic until soft. Stir in the soy sauce, brandy, thyme, and pepper. Remove from the heat and allow to cool slightly. Add the sour cream and puree the mixture in a blender or food processor; it should still have some texture and not be completely smooth. Press into a suitable dish or pot and pour melted butter to cover the top. Add a few additional sprigs of fresh thyme and refrigerate for 24 hours.

Vegetable Coconut Curry

SERVES 4 AS A MAIN COURSE

This light and creamy vegan curry is warmed with the golden blessings of turmeric, a spice sacred to Kali. This curry is extremely flexible in that it can be made with just

about any vegetables you have on hand—use sweet potatoes instead of white potatoes, for example, or replace the spinach with other green leaves. You do need to make the curry base first, so I have divided this recipe into two parts. The curry base can also be used for non-vegetarian curries as well, such as chicken, pork, and shrimp.

Curry Sauce

- **4 tablespoons vegetable oil**
- **1 medium onion, chopped**
- **3 garlic cloves, finely chopped**
- **3 tablespoons grated fresh ginger**
- **½ teaspoon cayenne pepper**
- **1 teaspoon ground turmeric**
- **½ teaspoon ground cumin**
- **1 teaspoon garam masala**
- **2½ cups vegetable broth or water**
- **2 or 3 tomatoes, peeled and chopped**

Heat the oil in a large, deep frying pan, and sauté the onions, garlic, and ginger until golden and fragrant. Stir in the dry spices and stir to make a paste. Then add the vegetable broth or water and the tomatoes and simmer for 25 minutes or until the sauce has thickened a little. Remove from the heat.

Vegetables

- **2 tablespoons vegetable oil**
- **4 or 5 potatoes, peeled and cut into small chunks**
- **2 large onions, sliced**
- **A bunch of fresh spinach leaves**
- **1 cup coconut milk or cream**
- **½ teaspoon salt**
- **1 small red chili, sliced**
- **A handful of fresh cilantro (coriander) leaves, chopped**

Heat the vegetable oil in a large frying pan or wok and fry the potatoes and onions until the potatoes are golden brown. Tear the spinach leaves into large pieces and add to the pan, stir-frying briefly. Add the coconut milk/cream, salt, and the curry sauce; simmer until the vegetables are soft. Lastly, stir in the sliced chili and generous quantities of fresh cilantro. Serve hot with lots of rice or bread to mop up the delicious and aromatic sauce.

Pakoras

MAKES 15–20 PAKORAS

These little vegetable fritters are traditional to Hindu cuisine. They make a lovely starter for an Indian feast or serve them as a snack. You will need chickpea or gram flour, also known as besan; it's generally available at larger supermarkets and whole food stores. In a pinch you can use ordinary

flour, but the taste will be a little different; in that case, add a little ground turmeric to the flour. This will give it a more traditional golden color.

> 1 cup chickpea flour
> ½ teaspoon baking soda
> Cold water
> 1 onion, peeled and thinly sliced
> 2 small potatoes, peeled and finely chopped
> 1 green chili, chopped (optional)
> 1 clove garlic, crushed
> ½ teaspoon ground cumin
> ½ teaspoon cayenne pepper
> ¼ teaspoon ground coriander
> 1 tablespoon chopped fresh cilantro (coriander) leaves
> ½ teaspoon salt
> Vegetable oil for frying

In a large bowl, combine the flour and baking soda and add enough cold water to make a thick, smooth batter. Stir in the onion, potatoes, and all the spices.

Heat vegetable oil in a deep frying pan or wok—the oil should be at least 1½ inches deep. Scoop up spoonfuls of the batter and drop into the hot oil. Don't cook too many at once, and fry for around 10 minutes, turning frequently, until the pakoras are crisp and golden brown. Drain well and serve warm or cold with the yogurt dip below or any kind of spicy chutney you like.

Spicy Mint Dip

Place 1 cup plain or Greek yogurt in a bowl and stir in 2 tablespoons chopped fresh mint, 1 teaspoon ground cumin, and ½ teaspoon each salt and cayenne pepper. Add a little cold water if necessary to make a smooth dipping sauce. Store in the fridge until serving.

Tiramisu

SERVES 8

I could never *not* include some version of this dessert in a book of food—a tribute to my Italian heritage, it's also simple and delicious, both to make and eat! The name means "pick me up" in Italian, and it's very appropriate. Coffee—what can one say? It's such a wonderful, energetic beverage (in moderation, of course) that gives us not only a boost of energy but is also linked to creative thought, clarity of spirit, and protection.

24 ladyfinger biscuits

1 cup strong coffee, cooled

2 tablespoons plus ¼ cup sugar, divided

2 tablespoons brandy (or coffee liqueur)

2 eggs, separated

8 ounces mascarpone cheese

½ teaspoon vanilla extract

Espresso powder and flaked almonds for garnish

218

You will need a square or rectangular baking or glass dish that fits two layers of the biscuits snugly. Mix the coffee, 2 tablespoons sugar, and brandy together and set aside.

Beat the egg yolks with ¼ cup sugar until thick and soft, then carefully fold in the mascarpone cheese to make a smooth mixture. Add the vanilla. Beat the egg whites in a grease-free glass bowl until they are stiff but not dry and fold into the cheese mixture. Dip the biscuits quickly in the coffee mixture (they must not be saturated) and arrange one layer of biscuits in the dish. Spoon over half the cheese mixture and spread out to cover the biscuits. Repeat with a second layer of biscuits and the remaining cheese. Sprinkle with espresso powder and flaked almonds. Chill for at least 2 hours before serving.

Corn Waffles

SERVES 4–6

Corn, in all its incarnations, has been used as an offering to the earth gods over the ages. It's been a part of harvest celebrations for centuries, as well as being an important part of fertility and abundance rituals. These corn waffles are a lovely way of ensuring luck and abundance at this harvest season, and they just taste great. If you don't have a waffle maker, they can also be made as small pancakes.

Serve topped with crispy bacon, honey, fresh fruit, cheese, or anything else you like at your magical harvest breakfast or brunch.

> **4 eggs, separated**
> **½ cup vegetable oil**
> **1 cup plain yogurt or buttermilk**
> **1½ cups self-rising flour (see recipe on page 30)**
> **1 teaspoon salt**
> **¾ cup sweet corn**

Beat the egg whites in a grease-free glass bowl until they are stiff but not dry and set aside. In a large bowl, beat the egg yolks with the oil and yogurt, then add the flour and salt and beat to make a smooth batter. Stir in the sweet corn, then fold in the egg whites. Heat your waffle maker following the instructions and cook the waffles. Alternatively, fry large spoonfuls of the mixture in shallow oil until crispy and golden brown. Drain well on paper towels. Serve fresh and warm.

PANTRY

Spicy Apple Chutney

MAKES ABOUT FOUR 4-OUNCE JARS

Apples again—beloved of gods and goddesses from Apollo to Freya, Hercules to Pomona. And this simple recipe can be made using just about any apple, even those windfalls that are a little less than perfect, making it an ideal recipe for frugal kitchen witches. This chutney makes the perfect accompaniment to roast meats or barbecued dishes; it also goes exceptionally well with a simple meal of bread and cheese.

> 1½ pounds apples, peeled, cored, and chopped
> 2 or 3 large onions, peeled and chopped
> 2 garlic cloves, crushed
> 2 tablespoons fresh ginger
> 2 cups cider vinegar
> 1 cup brown sugar
> 2 teaspoons salt
> 1 teaspoon yellow mustard seeds

1 teaspoon cinnamon

1 teaspoon nutmeg

½ teaspoon cayenne pepper (optional)

½ cup yellow raisins

Combine all but the yellow raisins in a large heavy-bottomed saucepan and simmer gently over low heat, stirring frequently, until the mixture is thick and soft, although the apples should still have a little texture. Cool, stir in the raisins, and then spoon into small sterilized jars and seal. This chutney keeps well in a cool, dark place but should be stored in the fridge once it's opened.

Morning Clarity Tea

I love having a little jar of this tea blend tucked away in my pantry. As the year starts to turn towards the dark, it reminds me of the changes we all need to go through and embrace and the power we have to grow in any season and at any time. It's based on an old Moroccan tea recipe and is lovely served in the early morning as a kind of sunrise benediction.

1 cup black tea leaves

1 teaspoon dried mint leaves

½ teaspoon ground ginger

½ teaspoon ground cinnamon

¼ teaspoon ground coriander

¼ teaspoon ground cardamom

2 or 3 whole cloves

A few dried rose petals (optional)

Combine all the ingredients and then store in a tightly covered jar or tin in a cool and dark place. To make the tea, simply place 2 teaspoons of the tea mixture in a cup or mug and cover with boiling water. Leave to steep for 10 minutes, then strain and drink—with a little honey added if you prefer some sweetness. A sprig of fresh mint is also a lovely garnish for this gently uplifting drink.

There is a land of the living and a land of the dead and the bridge is love, the only survival, the only meaning.

Thornton Wilder

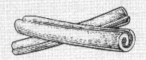

OCTOBER

Magic, Memory, and Spirits

Samhain marks the first—and for many the most significant—of the major festivals in the Celtic year. Although recently it often seems to be overshadowed by Halloween and its rather overdone commercial facets, the fact remains that this is an extremely significant and magical time of the year on many levels, both in the kitchen and beyond.

The time is coming to shift from the light to the dark, both in the physical world as leaves fall, light fades, and winter sets in, but also in our own lives and beings. This is a time for us to learn to be still, dig deep, and discover our intuitive soul and spirit. Sometimes, as lightly as the bright leaves fall from the trees, this may teach us to let go of things that no longer serve nor empower us. Yet this is also a time of mysteries, a moment when the veil becomes thin and we can truly see, feel, and experience other worlds, a time when we are closest to those who have gone before us into the light and shining places.

The alchemy of Samhain is very present in our kitchens, for the foods we prepare and eat form a major part of our personal memories and story, and it's in these recipes and meals that we often find a sacred connection to those lost to us on the physical plane. Samhain is about honoring these connections in a way that is meaningful to us personally. I don't care much for the decorations now typical of Halloween, but I find great joy in the creation of meals that remind me of my much-loved spirit companions.

I grew up in Africa, where much importance is given to the role of the ancestors in every aspect of peoples' lives. Their opinion and approval is sought for most life decisions and changes, such as marriage and death, and no less so than with meals, which are often prepared specifically to please (or appease) the ancestors.

At this time we, too, can remember with love and honor those who once shared our table, and allow the food we prepare to bring us closer to loved ones who are no longer

with us on the physical plane. Food brings us closer to those gone into the light, so I find preparing and cooking dishes and meals at Samhain that remind me of a particular person or time a truly sacred ritual, whether I am alone or sharing this meal with others.

Morgan le Fey

There are several goddesses linked with this magical time of year, among them Hecate, Cerridwen, and the Morrigan, but my particular favorite is Morgan le Fey, also known as Morgana. Like these goddesses, she is linked with darkness, death, and the underworld, and like them she also represents so much more than that, including the duality that lives in each and every one of us. We all possess dark and light, fear and forgiveness, and loss and opportunity in equal measure, and the time of Samhain reminds us in a powerful way that unless we learn to embrace this duality, we will never become truly complete and whole.

Morgana is inextricably linked to the legend of King Arthur of the Round Table; in many legends she is named as his half sister and in others as his mistress. Gifted in magic and the use of herbs, she was part of a sinister plot to overthrow the king led by his vengeful nephew Mordred. Yet, after the battle, when King Arthur lay mortally wounded, it was Morgan le Fey who took him in a black

227

boat to the legendary Isle of Avalon (often seen as the otherworld); it is said that she tends him there to this day, with other fairy queens and goddesses, and that one day he will be healed and return to lead his people.

At Samhain Morgana reminds us that we need not fear the darkness; we need only be open to it and see beyond it to the lessons we can yet learn. She teaches us that there is redemptive power and healing when we move beyond hate to love and understanding. I believe this was a lesson she herself learned in Avalon, and so I often invoke her at this time (and others), particularly when I am struggling with any particular issues in my life or battling to understand losses and grief.

I have a small card with beautiful artwork of Morgan le Fey that I often place on my kitchen altar in this time; I also use it as part of the simple Samhain ritual below. (You can use other goddesses for this ritual, too—we all have our own individual spirits that speak to us on a deep level.)

Fill a dark glass bowl with water and place in the center of the table or worktop. Arrange candles around the bowl—I like to use white or silver because they seem to me to be the most magical. Do this ritual quietly, when it's already completely dark, and turn out any lights apart from the candles. Take a bunch of rosemary, fresh or dried, and

stir the surface of the water three times clockwise and three times anticlockwise. Then gaze into the water and quietly say the following words:

> *Tonight I remember. I remember those who*
> *have gone before me, those I no longer see*
> *except in spirit and heart. I know and believe*
> *they rest in safety and light, and continue to*
> *guide and protect me as I travel along this path*
> *of life. May I always be open to their quiet*
> *whispers and soul words; may I never forget.*
> *May I never forget my own power and magic,*
> *my own light and darkness, for one cannot*
> *exist without the other. May I never fear the*
> *darkness but embrace it and see it for the gift*
> *it is, the spirit gift, the gift of understanding.*
> *I am here, and all is well. And so it is.*

Often, while or after doing this ritual, I have been left with a powerful sense of others being beside me, of their presence and love; it's a wonderful experience and one that I hope will come to you, too, if you choose to do this with absolute openness and a receptive spirit.

My Little Magic Broom

While I have a practical kitchen broom that I use every day for sweeping up spills and crumbs in my kitchen, I also have a lovely little magic broom—maybe the kind only a good witch would use! Brooms are a powerful form of kitchen magic, and one that really helps when life is becoming a little more than we can handle or we feel that either our space or we ourselves need some additional protection.

My little broom was created by a Zulu craftsman and only measures about 12 inches in length. It has a sturdy wooden handle around which I have wrapped some purple ribbon (just because purple is my favorite color, and to me it represents both insight and protection). I have also added a few thin white and silver cords strung with small amethyst and crystal beads. This broom hangs on a hook near my back door. When I need it, I use it on my kitchen surfaces or around the doors, sweeping anticlockwise and saying the following simple incantation:

> *Blessed and protected, all harm swept*
> *away—only light and joy may enter*
> *here, now and in the future.*

After using the broom, I sprinkle it with a little sea water and a few drops of lavender oil to both freshen and empower it.

The Enchanted Table

Every kitchen should have a table, even if it's quite small. I don't think a kitchen can really work its best magic without a table for people to sit at, eat on, share stories and confidences at, and so much more. If the kitchen is the heart of the home, then the table is the heart of the kitchen. It's a place where the stories of our lives can unfold, where we can remember who we are and where we come from, where we can celebrate and laugh and sometimes cry if we need to.

I lived on a farm once that had an enormous kitchen and a very large table; it could probably have seated sixteen people in a pinch. That table was old and a bit dented, but it was the most beautiful thing in the kitchen, apart from the black iron wood-burning stove. (There was no electricity on the farm, and we used oil lamps for light.) I loved that table. I sat at it every morning with the day's first cup of coffee to plan what I was going to do and—more importantly—what I was going to cook. In the middle of the table was a large wooden bowl in which I kept vegetables and herbs gathered from the garden, and next to it sat a little wire basket of freshly laid eggs. I had a jug of wildflowers too, and I kept my tarot and oracle cards in a little bag on the table so I always had a moment to reflect and dream while the food was cooking.

The farm and that table live on in my memory, even though sadly I can never return there—but they both taught me such magical lessons about the simple sharing of good things. I hope you will also have a table like that (if you don't already) and that you will honor it through the seasons and times you spend around it. It may sound obvious, but keep your table fairly clean and tidy—don't allow it to become a second junk drawer where people just pile stuff. Wipe and polish it as needed.

Cleansing and Protective Surface Wash

Bless your table and other kitchen surfaces by sprinkling with this cleansing and protective wash: place a handful of fresh rosemary sprigs, sage, thyme, and basil in a large glass bowl together with a clove of garlic and a teaspoon of fennel or dill seeds. Pour over 2 cups of boiling water and allow the herbs to infuse for at least an hour. When the liquid is cool, strain it and place it in a glass spray bottle with ½ cup white vinegar.

Kitchen Pleasures

- Do you have special plates, glasses, dishes, or table linens that were handed down to you and remind you of times past and meals shared? Don't let them sit in cupboards gathering dust. Use them with joy and thankfulness this October, remembering those whose touch and memory still linger ...

- If you can get hold of truffles, these precious nuggets with their magical earthiness, use a little shaved or grated truffle in sauces, butters, or egg dishes. You can also make a very special oil for cooking by placing a few truffle shavings in a small bottle of olive oil and allowing it to steep for at least a month.

- Make lunar tea to access the prophetic magic of the moon. Simply make your favorite herbal tea and stand it in the moonlight for a little while before drinking it quietly in the dark. Allow feelings and emotions to come up as you sip the brew, and welcome them and their lessons.

◆ Create a little psychic protection and cleansing pot in your kitchen by combining some dried rosemary, thyme, bay leaves, basil, and a single star anise in a small jar. Add a sprinkling of sea salt and a small jade, amethyst, or turquoise stone for protection. Keep the jar on your altar or kitchen table and allow its protective qualities to bless you at this sacred time.

RECIPES

Cinderella Soup

MAKES 4–6 MEDIUM SERVINGS

Pumpkins are obviously connected with both Halloween and Samhain, and they are a powerful tool in witchy magic. Maybe if Cinderella had eaten this soup, she wouldn't have needed the glass slippers to catch the man of her dreams. Seriously, though: pumpkins have major good vibes and help bring abundance and prosperity. You can use just about any kind of pumpkin in this recipe, but I like butternut for its sweet flavor.

This recipe is a bit different than many others in that it includes tomatoes; they give an extra burst of flavor and add to the soup's rich color. Made with vegetable broth, this also makes a wonderful vegetarian or vegan meal served with nut or seed bread.

¼ cup olive oil

2 pounds pumpkin, peeled, seeded, and
    cut into cubes

2 leeks or onions, sliced thinly

1 large carrot, sliced

4 garlic cloves, crushed

2 tomatoes, peeled and chopped

1 red chili, sliced

Fresh oregano or thyme to taste

2 bay leaves

6 cups vegetable or chicken broth

Salt and pepper to taste

Heat the olive oil in a large, deep saucepan and fry the pumpkin, leeks, carrot, and garlic together until softened. Add the remaining ingredients and simmer gently until the vegetables are tender. Remove the bay leaves, cool the mixture slightly, and then put two-thirds of the soup in a blender or food processor and blend until smooth. (Don't blend all of it since the soup is nicest when it still has a bit of texture!) Return to the pot and heat the soup again; season with salt and pepper to taste. Sprinkle with a little more finely chopped oregano or thyme before serving with crusty bread.

Beef Niçoise Pie

SERVES 6

Bright, rich flavors celebrate the feast of Samhain on so many levels—a gathering of soul and spirit and tastes that remind us of home and memory. I have added a simple spoon-over pastry to this dish to make it a meal-in-one, but you can leave it off and simply serve the casserole with potatoes, rice, or the sweet potato dish below. Beef is linked to fire and masculine energy, while the orange traditionally added to this dish is also sacred to fire, earth gods, and purification.

It is possible to make this entirely on top of the stove in a suitable heavy casserole dish, but I find it easier to make it in the oven. You can also use a slow cooker, which works wonderfully, although you will have to finish the pastry in the oven if you are adding it.

> **5 pounds boneless beef (I like using rump)**
> **2 tablespoons flour**
> **Salt and pepper to taste**
> **3 tablespoons olive oil**
> **1 tablespoon dried thyme plus 2 bay leaves**
> **½ pound small white or pickling onions**
> **4 ounces lean bacon, cut into dice**
> **2 small carrots, sliced**
> **2 garlic cloves, crushed**

3 tablespoons brandy

2 cups red wine

1 cup beef broth

Juice and rind of 1 orange

2 tablespoons tomato puree

Fresh thyme sprigs and 2 tablespoons black or
green olives, stoned and sliced, for garnish
(optional)

Preheat oven to 350°F.

Cut the beef into 1-inch cubes. Mix the flour, salt, and pepper on a plate and dust the beef with this seasoned flour. Heat the olive oil in a large Dutch oven and fry the meat in batches until it is lightly browned. Remove from the pan. Add the dried herbs, onions, bacon, carrots, and garlic to the oil and fry until they are soft and golden. Return the beef to the pan and pour in the brandy, wine, beef broth, orange juice and rind, and tomato puree. Cover the dish and place in the preheated oven for at least 2 hours or until the meat is soft. Remove the bay leaves and thicken the sauce, if necessary, with a little flour mixed with water.

If you are serving this dish without the pastry topping, stir in the olives and garnish with a few fresh thyme sprigs.

Pour-Over Pastry

This is actually an old South African recipe called *Skep-Kors*, which translates literally as "scoop crust." It makes a delicious topping for this aromatic beef casserole and is far easier and quicker to make than regular pie crust. Beat 2 eggs, ½ cup vegetable oil, and 1 cup milk together well, then fold in 1½ cups flour, 1 teaspoon baking powder, and a pinch of salt. Beat very well to form a thick, smooth batter. Remove the casserole dish from the oven after about 1¾ hours and spoon the batter over the top of the meat—it will spread out to form a crust. Bake another 25 or 30 minutes; the top of the pie should be golden brown and a little risen. Remove from the oven, let the dish stand for 10 minutes, and serve.

Spicy Baked Sweet Potatoes
SERVES 4–6

A warming fall side dish with the previous beef pie recipe, this is also delicious with other meat or chicken casseroles or even just on its own. Only a little chili is used, so the dish is not overly spicy—but you can add more if you want to increase the heat factor a bit. This is a lovely recipe for Samhain, with magical properties for grounding and psychic insight.

Preheat oven to 400°F.

1½ **pounds sweet potatoes**

4 or 5 scallions

4 garlic cloves, crushed

1 or 2 small green chilies

4 tablespoons olive oil, divided

1 teaspoon dried thyme

Salt to taste

A few sprigs of fresh rosemary

Peel the sweet potatoes and cut them into wedges or thick slices. Slice the scallions thickly. Chop the chilies, removing the seeds if you prefer a little less heat. Put 2 tablespoons of the olive oil in a large roasting pan and arrange the potatoes, scallions, garlic, and chilies on top.

Sprinkle over the remaining olive oil, dried thyme, and salt to taste. Bake 40 to 50 minutes or until the potatoes are softened and golden brown. (Add a little extra oil or water if they seem to be drying out.) Serve the dish warm, sprinkled with some fresh rosemary.

Fall Harvest Salad

SERVES 6 GENEROUSLY AS A SIDE DISH

A beautiful, bountiful salad for fall feasting, packed with symbolism for the autumn equinox and Samhain. Apples have been renowned for their magical qualities through the centuries, and in Celtic wisdom it is believed that apple

trees mark the gateway between this world and the one of the spirits. Lettuce, too, is a portal for astral travel and spirit worlds, and watercress is loaded with feminine and protective energies. This colorful dish also includes pomegranates, which are sacred to both Persephone and Ceres, and as such are linked to death and rebirth. By the way, if you really cannot abide the taste of blue cheese, feel free to substitute crumbled feta instead.

1 head red lettuce

1 head curly green lettuce

2 Red Delicious apples

A handful of fresh watercress

½ cup toasted pecans, chopped

4 ounces blue cheese, crumbled

½ cup light olive (or vegetable) oil

¼ cup white wine vinegar

1 tablespoon minced green onion

2 tablespoons lemon juice

1 tablespoon honey

Salt and pepper to taste

2 tablespoons pomegranate seeds

In a large, beautiful bowl, arrange the torn lettuce leaves. Core the apples, slice thinly, and place on top of the lettuce. Sprinkle with the watercress, toasted pecans, and cheese. Make the dressing by combining the remaining

241

ingredients (apart from the pomegranate seeds) in a small bowl or jug and whisking together well. Pour the dressing over the salad and sprinkle with the pomegranate seeds. Chill for 30 minutes and serve. It's best not to make this salad too far ahead of time, as the apple slices might start to go brown.

Funnel Cakes

Beloved treat of festivals and fairs, funnel cakes are easy to make at home and are a yummy Halloween snack. The only problem with this recipe is making enough to satisfy the demand! By the way, although you can use a funnel (obviously) to drizzle the batter into the oil, I tend to use an empty, clean mustard sauce bottle with a spout—it's easier to control and less messy.

> 2 cups milk
>
> 1 egg, beaten
>
> 1 teaspoon vanilla extract
>
> 2 cups flour
>
> ¾ cup sugar
>
> 1 teaspoon baking powder
>
> ½ teaspoon salt
>
> 4 tablespoons melted butter
>
> Vegetable oil for frying
>
> Confectioners' sugar

242

Beat the milk, egg, and vanilla together in a large bowl. In another bowl, sift the flour, sugar, baking powder, and salt, then add to the milk mixture and beat well to form a smooth batter. Fold in the melted butter.

Pour the batter into a suitable container (see suggestion above). Heat oil in a deep frying pan—I often use my wok. The oil should be at least 1 inch deep and not too hot, otherwise the cakes will burn on the outside while still being uncooked inside. Drizzle concentric circles of batter into the oil, making 4 or 5 at a time. Fry, turning occasionally, until the funnel cakes are crispy, puffed up, and golden. Drain well on paper towels (kitchen paper) and serve warm, if possible, sprinkled liberally with confectioners' sugar. (Quantities are difficult to give, as it depends on the size of the cakes you make.)

PANTRY

Sweet and Spicy Nuts

MAKES 2 MEDIUM-SIZED JARS

Absolutely essential for this time of year both to serve to guests or simply to nibble furtively out of the jar when no one is looking. With their subtle warmth and spice, these nuts are addictive; use any of your favorites. I tend to use a combination of cashews, macadamias, pecans, and almonds.

Preheat oven to 350°F. Line a baking sheet with parchment (baking) paper.

> **10 ounces mixed nuts**
> **2 tablespoons olive oil**
> **1 teaspoon salt**
> **1 tablespoon brown sugar**
> **½ teaspoon cayenne pepper**
> **Pinch of ground cumin**

Place the nuts in a bowl and stir in the remaining ingredients. Mix well, then spread the nut mixture out on the prepared baking sheet. Bake 5 minutes, then stir well. Continue baking for another 10 minutes or until the nuts are toasted and golden. Remove from the oven, cool, and store in airtight containers or jars.

Rocky Road Popcorn

MAKES ABOUT 4 OR 5 CUPS

These sweet and sticky Samhain or Halloween treats are for children and the young at heart; these tastes never seem to lose their magic! I like to shape this mixture into smallish balls that can be stored in cellophane bags and trimmed with bright ribbons. The popcorn will keep for a week or so if stored airtight.

> **4 ounces popping corn**
> **4 ounces mini marshmallows**
> **1 cup chopped pecans (optional)**
> **1 cup chocolate chips**
> **1 stick butter**
> **1 cup sugar**
> **¼ cup light cream**
> **1 teaspoon vanilla extract**
> **¼ teaspoon salt**

Pop the corn and allow it to cool, then spread it on a large lined baking sheet. Sprinkle the marshmallows, nuts, and chocolate chips on top; mix well.

In a small saucepan, melt the butter and sugar together until the mixture is thick and smooth. Stir in the cream and cook for a few minutes to make a caramel sauce. Stir in the vanilla and salt. Remove from the heat, cool for a few minutes, then pour the sauce over the popcorn mixture, tossing it lightly. Some of the chocolate chips and marshmallows might melt a bit, but that's okay.

Cool the mixture completely, then shape it into balls and store in airtight containers or sealed packets.

Dining with one's friends and beloved family is certainly one of life's primal and most innocent delights, one that is both soul-satisfying and eternal.

Julia Child

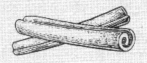

NOVEMBER

Gratitude, Sharing, and Ceremony

November is the very beginning of the winter tide, and as such it can be quite challenging for those of us who don't particularly enjoy the cold, dark months that lie ahead. But, as with everything in our lives, we can shift our focus from one of regret to one of thanks and celebration.

Winter starts with celebrations, particularly if you live in the United States, where Thanksgiving is one of the major holidays of the year. Perhaps it's a holiday we should all embrace, in our own time and way, for giving thanks and gratitude are the cornerstones for creating a truly abundant life. If we constantly focus on the problems in our lives and on what we don't have, we restrict our capacity for both happiness and growth.

Winter is also the time to start looking inward, even in the midst of holiday celebrations, and giving ourselves quiet time and space to reflect on the year that is almost gone and think about our intentions for the future. Sun energy is waning now, and we need the darker, more intuitive energy of the moon to guide us going forward as we retreat into the quiet, dark time that lies ahead.

However, in our kitchens there should be lots of light and warmth as we start to prepare increasingly warmer and more nourishing meals: soups, stews, hot drinks, and baked desserts. Foods are often cooked slowly or roasted at this time to make them easily digestible and bring out their nutritive qualities. It's a time, too, to celebrate all the meals we have shared over the years, and the healing and hope to be found around our kitchen tables.

A Menu of Memory

This time of year, when we usually gather together for celebration and thanks, is also a wonderful opportunity to work with our kitchen journals, remembering the meals shared and enjoyed over the years with friends and family.

I like to create a new "Menu of Memory" each November and write it down in my journal. For this menu, I choose a few dishes (starter or soup, main course, salad, bread, dessert) that remind me in a meaningful way of a time, place, and people loved and remembered. This can be both a joyful and emotional experience, especially if the dishes remind us of people no longer with us on the physical plane. I did this last year a few months after losing my mom, and I can honestly say this exercise was watered by a lot of tears, as well as bringing forth some sweet memories.

Write down what this menu means to you, as well as your memories of the people it honors; you might then choose to prepare this menu for a feast of thanksgiving and gratitude or simply make one of the dishes and share it with people you love. If you are on your own, prepare one of the dishes and eat it quietly and attentively at the table while thinking of the times and people it brings to mind. Keep a little of the dish aside and place it on a plate next to a white candle. Burn some sage, lavender, or rosemary incense as you quietly say the following blessing over the food:

I am blessed by this meal. I am blessed by
this memory. I invite you to share this meal
with me in spirit and heart. You remain
with me and always will. And so it is.

Cooking with Moon Rhythms

We can never move outside the powerful and beautiful influence of the moon and her magic. She is the source of so much energy and enchantment on this earth—from the tides to the seasons to our own bodies and emotional responses. The work we do in our kitchens as witches of hearth and home is no exception to this, and these unique energies can be harnessed in creative and intentional ways to nourish ourselves and those around us through the lunar cycle and year.

Following the path of the moon, here are some ideas for using these phases in the magical kitchen:

New or Dark Moon

A powerful time of the Dark Goddess, a time for inner work, divination, and spirit journeys. It is not a time for making elaborate meals or recipes that are heavy in any sense of the word. It is, rather, a time for planning what it is we want to create in our lives going forward on every level, and to do this effectively, we need to cook and eat lightly, with awareness of what nourishes and sustains us as we move on and what messages we are receiving from our bodies, especially if we are feeling unwell or depleted on any level.

Waxing Moon

A time to actively set dreams and intentions and work on making them manifest in our lives. It is time to try something new in the kitchen: different flavorings and ingredients to the ones we are used to—maybe a new range of warming spices and herbs. It's a time for actively seeking abundance and healing, so using lots of fruit and bright vegetables is appropriate for this moon phase as we work spells and rituals for ourselves and the greater good.

Full Moon

This is the time of abundance—of the earth and in our own lives—and we should celebrate and honor it with the fullness of the moon. It's time for feasting and sharing with those we love, for honoring the Hearth Goddess with lots of rich and delicious recipes with bright flavorings—spices and herbs should be used with gusto at the full moon! Use lots of chilies and spicy warmth, too, in the meals we prepare; it's also a good time to enjoy fruits, nuts, baked treats, and desserts.

Waning Moon

This is a time for stepping back and reflecting on what we need to hold on to and let go of; in the practical realm, this can include tidying up kitchen clutter and getting rid of old or unusable food—yes, I am talking about those

strange, unidentifiable things lurking in the back of the cupboard or at the bottom of the freezer! It's also a time to clear up emotional blocks and old patterns that may be preventing us from living truly free, clear, and magical lives. This time in the kitchen calls for bright, fresh citrus, lots of vegetables and herbs, garlic, and soups packed with simple goodness for our well-being.

The Enchantment of a Hygge Kitchen

It's been quite a few years since the Danish concept of *hygge* (pronounced "hoo-gah") became something of a buzzword, with numerous books and articles published about this concept—probably too many, in retrospect, for the whole idea became a little overblown.

But in essence, this is a simple concept and one which basically echoes the principles of our enchanted kitchens in so many ways. Norse in origin but adopted by the Danes over two hundred years ago as a way of dealing with their very long, cold, and dark winters, hygge is a way of finding and really enjoying the simple pleasures of life on a daily basis. Just the everyday things like light and warmth, delicious home baking, steaming hot drinks, the comfort of spending time with loved ones around the kitchen table ... these are part of the whole concept of hygge, just as they should be a part of our kitchen magic, especially

254

in November, as winter really sets in and we face a few months of frosty darkness and cold winds.

Some Ideas for Everyday Hygge Magic

- Our kitchens should, above all, be both warm and comfortable. Add some soft cushions to the kitchen chairs, and make sure there's a knitted throw or small quilt available to drape over cold feet.

- Meals don't have to be elaborate—even something as simple as sitting together and sharing cups of warm soup and bread or coffee and cake is perfect hygge magic. And, of course, there is the lovely Swedish tradition of fika—one which I wholeheartedly endorse! Basically, fika means taking a few breaks during the day to enjoy a cup of coffee or tea and a little something sweet—a few cookies or a slice of cake—as a welcome respite from the demands of the daily routine and, not incidentally, a chance to spend a few precious moments with loved ones and friends.

- Notice and savor each moment—which is really the general theme of this book anyway.

- Nature should be a part of the kitchen—and indeed of your home in general. Enjoy indoor plants, herbs in pots, a spray of dried flowers, or even just leaves in an old jug...

- Make a fire if possible; if not, use lots and lots of candles (white is fine) on windowsills or arranged down the center of your kitchen table. Make sure they can be burned safely, of course—setting your kitchen alight is definitely not going to increase your feelings of calm and relaxation! To add a natural note, you can also add a few simple found objects like shells, pebbles, or pieces of driftwood around the candles.

- Essential oils to add to candles or diffusers that are suitable for this mood include sandalwood, jasmine, lavender, bergamot, and ylang-ylang.

- Cookies and cakes are a big part of hygge. They don't have to be elaborate; simple and traditional recipes are generally the order of the day.

- In addition to coffee, tea, and hot chocolate, consider making mulled wines or ciders with the added warming benefits of cinnamon (a major hygge spice) and star anise.

Kitchen Pleasures

- November 13 is the day for celebrating the Roman goddesses Juno and Minerva, who are linked with grains, bread, and the harvest. Make a loaf of your favorite bread or try one of the recipes in this book. Better still, make a few loaves, wrap them beautifully, and give them away to those you love and cherish.

- Is there anything better than sitting around the kitchen table on a cold night with a big bowl of freshly popped corn (with a little salt and butter, of course)? You can also try making special popcorn recipes like the one on page 246.

- Bring fire into your kitchen and life by hanging a string of mixed red and green chili peppers in your kitchen. You can also make a wreath by bending wire into a circle and stringing the peppers onto it—it lasts for ages and makes a potent symbol of protection for the kitchen and all those within.

- Make a little bowl of this connection spice blend; you can sprinkle it around your kitchen or burn a small amount on an incense burner. Mix the dried and crumbled peel of an orange with ½ teaspoon each ground cloves and nutmeg and 1 teaspoon each ground cinnamon and dried thyme. This spice blend creates a warming and relaxing atmosphere, ideal for a happy and welcoming kitchen.

- At this time of gratitude and thanksgiving, remember the three gifts offered to the first settlers in North America by the Native Americans: corn, squash, and beans. Use them in your recipes or simply place a few kernels of corn and dried beans on your kitchen altar.

- Think soup in November—warming and nutritious, make a lot when you find a glut of winter vegetables and freeze it for later. A slow cooker is definitely the best when it comes to making soup, and it is one of the few appliances I really love and consider essential in my kitchen, the others being a blender and an electric mixer.

RECIPES

The Best Roast Chicken

SERVES 4–6

I think the term "comfort food" was created for this dish: it is just loaded with memories, both physical and emotional. Since no one in my family was particularly keen on turkey, this was usually a dish served for celebrations. Chickens have always been a symbol of sacrifice, dating back to Roman times, and they are still used for this in some cultures today; of course, they also symbolize fertility, well-being, and prosperity. This size chicken will feed 4–6 people, possibly with some leftovers—simply double the recipe if you are feeding a bigger crowd.

This dish goes so well with molehills (page 261): the soft potatoes make the perfect side to the succulent chicken and aromatic juices.

1 stick unsalted butter, softened

2 tablespoons olive oil

1 large chicken (2–3 pounds)

2 garlic cloves, crushed

1 handful each fresh thyme and sage,
   finely chopped

2 lemons

½ teaspoon salt

Freshly ground black pepper

1 cup dry white wine

Chicken broth

Preheat oven to 400°F. Grease a large roasting pan with a little oil.

Mix the butter and olive oil together, and then rub the mixture well all over the chicken. Rub the garlic over the chicken breasts, then sprinkle over the finely chopped thyme and sage. Cut the lemons in half and place the halves of one inside the chicken cavity. Squeeze the juice from the second lemon over the chicken, and then sprinkle with the salt and pepper to taste.

Place the chicken in the prepared roasting pan and carefully pour the wine around the chicken. Cover with aluminum foil and roast for about 25 minutes. Reduce the heat to 350°F, remove the foil, and continue roasting the chicken until it is cooked through and the skin is golden

brown and crisp. Add some chicken broth to the accumulated pan juices as the chicken cooks; you should have a fair amount of reduced and syrupy juice. Remove the lemons from the cavity and serve the chicken warm with the cooking juices spooned over it.

Molehills

SERVES 6

As in "don't make a mountain out of..."! Actually, it's perfectly possible to make a meal out of these delicious potato mounds, which are really just a fancy way of serving mashed potatoes; this proves, once again, that simple foods are often the most magical!

This dish goes wonderfully well with just about any main course, especially roast poultry or meats. Grounding energy comes from the potatoes, of course, while the cheese is loaded with positive vibes and general happiness. Did you know that cheese is one of our most ancient foodstuffs—and it's sacred to the Greek god Apollo? I like to use a strong Cheddar or something similar for this dish, which gives it a nice burst of extra flavor.

6 large potatoes

½ stick butter

½ cup milk

Salt and pepper to taste

1 cup whipping cream or milk

¾ cup grated Cheddar

Chopped chives (optional)

Peel the potatoes, cut them into chunks, and boil in salted water until soft. Drain, cool slightly, and then stir in the butter, milk, and salt and pepper to taste. Mash very well with a fork, potato masher, or blender; the potato mixture should be light and fluffy.

Preheat the oven to 350°F. Grease a square baking pan well. Using two spoons or an ice cream scoop, form mounds of the potato mixture and arrange in the pan, just touching each other. Carefully pour the cream over the mounds, then sprinkle on the grated cheese and chives. Bake 20 to 30 minutes or until the cheese has melted and the tops of the molehills are light golden brown. Serve hot.

Creamy Grape and Feta Salad

SERVES 4–6

A cool and crisp counterpart to the rich meals of this time of thanksgiving and gratitude! Grapes are a symbol of abundance and harvest and have been so since antiquity. They are also linked to the moon, so they can form part of any moon magic rituals—and I am not just talking about pouring a lovely glass of wine in the moonlight!

2–3 cups mixed salad leaves of your choice

1 cup red or white seedless grapes

½ cup chopped scallions

½ cup walnut halves

4 ounces feta cheese, crumbled

4 teaspoons Dijon mustard

1 tablespoon cider vinegar

½ cup single cream

Salt and pepper to taste

Arrange the salad leaves on a serving platter; sprinkle over the grapes, scallions, walnuts, and cheese. To make the dressing, combine the mustard and vinegar, then gradually whisk in the cream to make a smooth mixture. Add salt and pepper to taste. Pour the dressing over the salad just before serving.

Snow Moon Pie

SERVES 4–6

"There is a moon inside every human, and we need to be friends with it." So said Rumi, the wonderfully wise thirteenth-century Persian poet. Known as Frost Moon or Snow Moon in Native American tradition, the full moon in November heralds a time of special magic, of remembering our wild nature in the time of the dark and cold. Serve this special dessert to loved ones and friends, and remember that power and beauty are always ours, even on the frozen days.

This pie has its origins in a very old dessert my mother used to make called Snow Falls in Dark Woods; the name is fairly self-explanatory.

> 1½ cups chocolate cookies
> ½ cup butter, melted
> 2 egg yolks, room temperature
> ¼ cup superfine sugar
> Pinch of salt
> ½ teaspoon vanilla extract
> 2 tablespoons whiskey (optional)
> 2 cups whole milk
> 2 tablespoons gelatin
> 1 cup heavy cream

Preheat the oven to 350°F and grease a 9-inch pie pan with butter.

Crush the cookies very fine or use a food processor, then combine with melted butter and press into the prepared pie pan. Bake 10 minutes, then remove from the oven and cool completely before adding the filling.

To make the filling, beat the egg yolks, sugar, and a pinch of salt together until very thick and pale yellow in color. Stir in the vanilla and whiskey. In a large saucepan (or, preferably, a double boiler), heat the milk until just starting to simmer, then reduce heat and add the egg mixture, stirring continuously until the mixture thickens like custard; don't allow it to boil. Meanwhile, dissolve the gelatin in ¼ cup cold water over a dish of hot water. Stir the gelatin mixture into the custard and mix well. Lastly, whip the cream until stiff and fold it into the cooled custard. Spoon into the crumb crust and chill well before serving. I like to sprinkle more cookie crumbs over the top of the pie or, for a more magical effect, some edible sparkling glitter.

Almond Bars

MAKES 12–16 BARS

Another simple yet delicious cookie/bar recipe perfect for sharing at this time and inspired by traditional Italian Florentines but easier to make. You can add some chopped

cherries, raisins, or pecans to the topping if you like, but I prefer the simplicity of the almond topping with its magical connections to prosperity, intuition, and passion.

> **1 cup flour**
> **2 tablespoons sugar**
> **½ teaspoon baking powder**
> **2 sticks butter, divided**
> **1 egg**
> **½ cup sugar**
> **1 teaspoon vanilla extract**
> **3 tablespoons light cream**
> **1 cup flaked almonds**

Preheat oven to 350°F. Grease a 9-inch square baking pan well.

Sift the flour, 2 tablespoons sugar, and baking powder together, then rub in 1 stick of butter until the mixture is like fine breadcrumbs. Stir in the egg and mix to form a soft dough. Press the dough out evenly in the prepared baking pan.

In a small saucepan, melt the other stick of butter, ½ cup sugar, vanilla, and cream together over a low heat until the mixture is smooth. Stir in the almonds. Pour this mixture over the base and bake 15 to 20 minutes or until the topping is golden brown. Cool in the pan; cut into bars or squares while still warm.

PANTRY

Chermoula

MAKES ABOUT 2 CUPS SAUCE

This spicy Moroccan sauce/relish brings a warmth to chilly November days with its bright, sunny flavors and the added benefit of the protection- and creativity-enhancing energies of both chilies and cilantro. Add a little to sauces, marinades, and just about anything—from grilled chicken to roast vegetables.

1½ cups fresh cilantro (coriander) leaves, chopped

1 cup fresh parsley, finely chopped

1 tablespoon crushed garlic

2 small red chilies, sliced

1 teaspoon paprika

1 teaspoon ground coriander

½ teaspoon ground cumin

½ cup fresh lemon juice

¾ cup olive or vegetable oil

Place all the ingredients (apart from the oil) in a blender or food processor and mix until a fairly smooth paste is formed. Slowly pour in the oil, creating a thick, smooth sauce—you might not need to use all the oil. Pour the chermoula into sterilized glass jars, cover tightly, and store in the fridge, where it will keep for at least a month.

Mixed Fruit Pickle

MAKES THREE OR FOUR 4-OUNCE JARS

This quick pickle is simplicity itself to make and lends itself to using whatever dried fruit you have on hand. I tend to use a mixture of raisins, golden raisins, cranberries, and dried apricots or peaches, finely chopped. Apart from the many fruit energies, vinegar is linked with fire and passion, as well as being powerful when it comes to getting rid of bad spells or negative forces in your life. You can also use honey or golden syrup in place of the light corn syrup.

> **1 pound mixed dried fruit (see above)**
> **1 onion, finely chopped**
> **2 garlic cloves, crushed**
> **½ teaspoon turmeric**
> **A pinch of cayenne pepper**
> **1 cup apple cider vinegar**
> **1 teaspoon grated cloves**
> **½ teaspoon black pepper**
> **½ cup light corn syrup**

Place the fruit in a large saucepan, and mix the onion, garlic, turmeric, and cayenne pepper in well. Pour over the remaining ingredients and simmer gently for about 10 minutes. Remove from the heat and cool thoroughly before bottling in small, sterilized glass jars.

The pickle will keep well for a few months in a cool, dry place. Store in the refrigerator once opened.

The present moment
is filled with joy
and happiness.
If you are attentive,
you will see it.

Thich Nhat Hanh

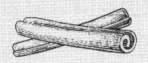

DECEMBER

Celebration, Rest, and Peace

Yule … the midwinter celebration (usually around December 21 in the northern hemisphere) marks not only the shortest day of the year, but also the beginning of the shift back from darkness to light, even if that's hard to imagine on these cold, short days. These days, obviously, the feast of Christmas—which borrows many of its traditions from Yule—has taken over in no small way and tends to dominate the month of December, but I believe we can and should give Yuletide its proper place in our kitchens, homes, and hearts.

Our kitchens at this time can be like cozy nests full of warmth, comfort, and security, the ideal antidote to the darkness and cold without. We can enjoy baking and simmering pots of stew or soup, and drinking cups of herbal tea while we chat, read, or listen to our favorite music. The kitchen can be colorful in a different way to the colors of summer, as we bring in the many shades of evergreens (fir, pine, holly) and the bright warming red of holly berries. Essential oils and scented candles can echo this warmth by using fragrances such as myrrh, frankincense, juniper, sweet orange, and sandalwood. Citrus fruits can be hung as pomanders or simply piled in wooden bowls; chili peppers and cranberries, too, lend bright warmth to the winter kitchen and can be added to wreaths and other decorations.

But this time of year also asks us—in the midst of all the celebrations and busy activity—to be still and give ourselves time to rest, in the same way as the earth is resting now and preparing herself for the spring. This can be difficult if there are lots of demands on our time and attention, but it's a vital part of this whole winter season.

It can also be helpful to reflect on what it is you love—and also don't really like—about this time of year. For example, I was raised to believe that "more is more" when it came to gift buying and giving, and until a few years ago I

went totally overboard when it came to buying gifts, which made little practical or financial sense. I was constantly stressing as to whether I had bought enough until, finally, I chose to step back from that and focus on a single gift (even something handcrafted) that is, hopefully, far more memorable in the long run.

Following on from this, how can you keep things simple, both practically and emotionally, especially if you are responsible for entertaining family and friends in the Yuletide season? After all, kitchen witches are nothing if not down to earth!

Food is obviously a big part of many people's celebrations, but feasts can be pared down and still be both delicious and memorable—it really isn't necessary to exhaust yourself and the budget, and I promise you that people will remember the warmth and joy you extend to them just as much without the elaborate meals. A nice option is to have a potluck celebratory meal, with everyone bringing one prearranged dish for the table.

Simplicity is always beautiful, and that includes the meals we prepare. Of course, this is the time of year for traditions, provided they make sense to you on a personal level. I have a couple of handwritten recipes from my mother's old recipe book stuck at the back of my journal;

these are recipes without which the festive season would seem incomplete to me, and I always try to make at least one or two of them.

This is the season when we celebrate the Norse goddess Freya: she who blesses love, beauty, family, joy, marriage, and motherhood. She's also a goddess of war and magical witchcraft, so she makes a powerful ally in the kitchen and elsewhere. Friday is her sacred day, but we can honor her any day by the meals and feasts we create and share. She's especially fond of dishes made with milk, apples, honey, strawberries, or pork. As the guardian goddess of cats, you might also consider donating some food or volunteer time to a cat refuge in December in her honor.

Above all, allow yourself to feel and express the magic of the midwinter season in whatever way works for you. Honor yourself—body, heart, and soul—at this special and enchanted time, and sparkle bright like the midwinter stars!

Welcoming the Sun

When the shift begins to occur back from darkness to light at this time, it's a wonderful opportunity to celebrate all we have been given through the year just past and enjoy our connections on every level. Traditionally, overnight

gatherings were held on the night of December 21, with people feasting and sharing until the first signs of the morning light. Obviously, this might not be entirely practical, depending on our individual circumstances and lifestyle, but we can still create a simple and meaningful ceremony—and the kitchen is the perfect place for doing this.

This does need to be planned a little ahead in terms of arranging a light meal or snacks and some warming drinks. If you are fairly abstemious or there are children in the group, consider some cider warmed with spices; alternatively, you can have a bowl of mulled wine or—my personal favorite—homemade or purchased eggnog.

Gather together around the kitchen table and give everyone a red candle (plus a lighter or matches). Burn some of your favorite incense (I like Nag Champa) or cleanse the group lightly with it, wafting the smoke over each participant. Sit quietly in the dark for a while, then give everyone in the room a chance to speak, if they so wish; perhaps they want to share a particular wish or hope they have at this time or their thoughts about the year now almost gone.

When everyone has spoken, ask them to light their candles and speaking either singly or as a group, say the following simple blessing:

Earth, you have given us both light and darkness. On this night we give thanks for the return of the sun and for the blessings of warmth and growth. The old year has passed away; the new year is here. May we all be blessed with light, with warmth, with grace. And so it is.

Arrange the candles in the center of the table and gather around to enjoy a simple feast, conversation, and companionship.

Your Kitchen Journal at Yuletide

Keeping a personal kitchen journal (aka grimoire, scrapbook, or commonplace book) offers us a safe, loving, and nonjudgmental place to record our lives on every level: from the practical to the spiritual, from recipes to rituals to memories. The very act of writing and committing words to paper somehow seems to open us up to our deepest selves in a healing way. Words are incredibly powerful!

In the dark, icy earth of the winter months, we can plant seeds that will develop into something new and beautiful; we can learn to be still and hold our thoughts and dreams in a gentle and safe place.

My mother, who was definitely something of a kitchen witch (although she would never have used the term) kept

a Christmas journal for several years when I was a child; recently, while going through her things after she passed away, I found one of these journals, dating from the 1970s. It was at once interesting and also bittersweet to read her recipes and plans for the holidays and look at the photos she had added to the pages, but it also reminded me of the importance of recording these moments in time as fragments of memory to be enjoyed and savored over the years.

Some suggestions for your Yuletide kitchen journal (although they are actually relevant all year through):

◆ Set aside a quiet time, preferably in both morning and evening (with no interruptions, if possible), to write in your kitchen journal. Make sure you feel relaxed and comfortable, perhaps with a fragrant candle burning and a cup of your favorite herbal tea at hand. Ground yourself, mentally and physically, and spend a little time reflecting on the day and what it is you need at this particular time. In the evening you might choose to reflect on the experiences of the day just past and what you have learned from them. What could you do to take better care of yourself while still being in the spirit of the season? How can you better connect with others and the world around you with love and appreciation? This can

be as simple as setting out a bowl of seeds and nuts for visitors to your winter garden.

- If the holiday season brings up particularly painful issues for you, as it sadly does for many of us, please feel free to write about them, and be totally honest—after all, no one will or should see what you write, unless you choose to share it. Perhaps there is a sense of loneliness or loss associated with this time of year, particularly if you are going through a period of grief or mourning. The first Christmas without my mother was painful on a number of levels, but writing down my feelings and memories helped me deal with this in a graceful way. Similarly, if there are aspects of this season that really push your buttons or people that make you dread this time, write this down and, most importantly, reflect on what you can do to either change the dynamics or cope with them in a way that is more healthy for your soul and spirit.

- What is it you are grateful for at this time? Especially now, when so many have experienced unprecedented loss on many levels, if we have a

home, food, warmth, and support—well, that is something to give thanks for. When we truly realize how blessed we are, our hearts and hands are open to receive even more blessings.

◆ You might choose to create some personally meaningful rituals before or after working on your kitchen journal that are particularly meaningful to you at this time. They can be as simple as having a cup of your favorite herbal tea blend or aromatic cappuccino. What matters is the creation of a ritual that works for you and inspires creative and peaceful thought.

◆ Burning scented candles, incense, or an oil diffuser are particular nice additions to your journaling time. I have a beautiful golden pillar candle, gifted to me by a friend, that is fragrant with both frankincense and juniper, which are very appropriate scents for this time of year. Other fragrance suggestions are rose, lavender, geranium, sandalwood, chamomile, cypress, bergamot, and orange. These particular oils are helpful when we are feeling anxious, stressed, tense, or exhausted at this time of year.

Kitchen Pleasures

- If you have any treasured old handwritten recipes, copy and laminate a few of them as very special Yuletide cards or simply keep them as page markers in your very favorite cookbooks.

- Brandy butter, a traditional Yuletide recipe from Britain, is usually served with hot Christmas pudding, but in my opinion just about any excuse will do! Mix 1 stick softened butter with enough confectioners' sugar to make a soft and creamy mixture, then stir in about 2 tablespoons brandy. Keep in the refrigerator and use with desserts or cake as a sauce or topping.

- Teatime in winter is a particularly special treat and way of celebrating the dark, cold days with warmth and good taste. Have a kitchen "high tea" with cakes, scones, cookies, sandwiches, and other savory snacks.

- December 13 marks the day of Little Yule, the earliest sunset, in Sweden. Celebrate this day by baking cakes or cookies flavored with cardamom.

- Decorate your kitchen with sprigs of rosemary and pine tied with red ribbons, symbols of immortality and blessings; these make a lovely natural place setting, too. For abundance and prosperity, create a simple kitchen wreath with holly leaves and berries, juniper, small pine cones, and a few cinnamon sticks, trimmed with a gold or green ribbon.

RECIPES

Roast Lamb with Herbs, Lemon, and Garlic

SERVES 6–8

A lamb roast is something quite special—certainly where I live it's not an everyday occurrence, given the cost, and perhaps that's a good thing. We need to have special days and feasts in the enchanted kitchen, times when we celebrate the gifts and bounty of the earth, as much as there are days when we eat grilled cheese sandwiches for supper.

This is, to me, the perfect Yule dish, full of lovely flavor and texture. You do preferably need to have a deboned leg of lamb, or you can use the shoulder, but it will feed fewer people—ask at your meat market. Although lamb is more traditionally linked with springtime festivities, I feel its connection to caring and nurturing energies and new beginnings are also perfect for this time of year, when we gather to celebrate and share, and also to look forward to the times yet to come.

2–3 pound leg of lamb, deboned

A handful each of rosemary, thyme, and parsley

2 garlic cloves, crushed

4 anchovy fillets, drained and chopped

1 teaspoon salt

2 tablespoons soft butter

¼ cup olive oil

2 tablespoons fresh lemon juice

1 cup dry white wine, divided

1 cup water

Lots of freshly ground pepper

Preheat oven to 150°F. Place the leg of lamb in a large and deep Dutch oven or similar oven dish. Chop the herbs finely, then add the garlic, anchovy, salt, and soft butter to form a paste. Spread this paste over the top and sides of the lamb. Mix the olive oil and lemon juice and pour it over the lamb. Pour over about half of the wine, cover the dish with foil, and roast for about 1½ hours.

Pour over the remaining wine and the water and continue to roast, uncovered, until the meat is very soft—this can take another hour or so, but because of the low oven temperature the meat will not dry out. However, you can spoon the pan juices over the lamb from time to time or add a little extra wine or water if needed. Slice or shred the meat onto warm plates and spoon some of the delicious pan juices over each serving.

Herb Roasted Vegetables

SERVES 6

Such a simple yet delicious dish that goes with just about anything and turns your Yule kitchen into a feast of aroma and flavor. The nicest thing about this recipe is that you can adapt it by using the winter vegetables you have on hand—and you can also use herbs to suit your particular magical intentions. The ones given here are just a suggestion—rosemary (for friendship, memory, and protection) and thyme (for courage, love, and healing). Perhaps you might prefer oregano for luck, parsley for purification, sage for wisdom and prosperity, or basil for creativity and joy. If you can't get fresh herbs, feel free to use dried ones, but obviously in lesser quantities.

Preheat oven to 400°F.

> **4 tablespoons olive oil, divided**
> **4 medium carrots**
> **2 small parsnips**
> **6 medium potatoes**
> **3 red onions**
> **1 red pepper**
> **1 garlic bulb**
> **A few fresh rosemary sprigs**
> **A handful of fresh thyme**
> **½ teaspoon salt**
> **Freshly ground black pepper**

285

Place 2 tablespoons of the oil in a large roasting pan. Peel the carrots, parsnips, potatoes, and onions, then cut them into thick slices or chunks. Cut the red pepper into thick strips, removing the seeds. Arrange the vegetables in the roasting pan, then peel the cloves of garlic and arrange them among the vegetables. Sprinkle the rosemary and thyme on top and drizzle the vegetables with the remaining olive oil. Season with the salt and black pepper to taste. Roast, uncovered, for 45 to 50 minutes or until the vegetables are softened and a little brown on top.

Serve hot or warm—you can even serve this as a simple winter main course, perhaps with a little crumbled feta or goat cheese over the top.

Spicy Pomander Salad

SERVES 4–6

Bright and warm flavors for the season, this recipe was inspired by one in the *Witch in the Kitchen* book by Cait Johnson. Of course, pomanders also used to be a traditional decoration and air freshener at this time of year; they were made using oranges, apples, or lemons studded with cloves (a fairly tedious process) and then hung up using bright ribbons or cord. Oranges are the fruit of happy, bright spirits and cloves are renowned for banishing

286

negative vibes and creating positive, warm, and abundant thoughts.

> **2–3 medium oranges**
>
> **2 cups red/green salad leaves**
>
> **1 small red onion, thinly sliced**
>
> **¼ cup olive oil**
>
> **¼ cup orange juice**
>
> **2 tablespoons lemon juice**
>
> **½ teaspoon ground cinnamon**
>
> **¼ teaspoon ground cloves**

Peel the oranges, removing all the white pith and seeds, then slice thinly. Arrange the salad leaves on a festive platter, then place the orange and onion slices on top. To make the dressing, whisk the olive oil with the remaining ingredients until the mixture is smooth. Pour it over the salad just before serving.

Baked Yuletide Pie with Ginger and Pecans
SERVES 6–8

When I was growing up, we always celebrated this season with the traditional Christmas pudding my mother made from scratch, using a recipe from her Scottish ancestors, which was full of all kinds of dried fruits and nuts. Its cooking process, which involved many hours of steaming on the stove, was long and tedious. So, in this bright

season, I would like to suggest this simpler yet equally delicious alternative that would make a fitting finale to any Yuletide feast.

Packed with the warming, healing, and powerful spiritual qualities of both dates and ginger, this dessert can be served with heavy cream or custard sauce or—my personal favorite—butter topping! You can add some finely chopped cherries, raisins, etc., to the batter if you want to ramp things up a little.

Preheat oven to 325°F.

Grease a deep 9-inch square or round baking pan well.

> 8 ounces pitted dates, chopped
> 1 teaspoon baking soda
> 1 cup boiling water
> 1 tablespoon preserved ginger, chopped
> ½ stick butter
> ½ cup brown sugar
> ½ cup molasses
> 1 egg
> 1½ cups flour, sifted
> 1 teaspoon baking powder
> 4 ounces chopped pecans
> 1 teaspoon vanilla extract

Place the dates in a small bowl, add the baking soda, and pour the boiling water over the dates. Leave for 10 min-

utes, then stir in the chopped ginger and allow the mixture to cool completely. In a large bowl, cream together the butter, brown sugar, and molasses until light and fluffy, then stir in the egg. Sift the flour and baking powder together and add to the butter mixture alternately with the cooled dates (including the liquid) and beat to form a smooth batter. Stir in the pecans and vanilla extract. Pour into the prepared pan and bake 50 to 60 minutes or until the mixture is well risen.

While it's cooking, prepare the butter topping: Melt ½ stick butter with ¼ cup each water and brown sugar, then stir in ¼ cup brandy (or rum, whiskey, or orange juice) and simmer for 5 minutes. Pour over the hot pie as soon as it comes out of the oven. Serve warm.

Moon and Stars Cookies

MAKES ABOUT 25–35 COOKIES

A plate of these pale gold cookies makes the perfect offering during this time of celebration and sharing. The lemon is sacred to the moon and brings all her magical power and gifts into these buttery cookies, while the lavender is also a gently protective herb for peace and love. You can omit the lavender if you prefer, but it does add a different taste dimension to these treats—just make sure it is very finely crumbled.

1 stick salted butter, softened

¾ cup superfine sugar plus ¼ cup extra

1 egg, separated

2 cups cake flour, sifted

Juice and zest of 1 lemon

1 teaspoon dried lavender, finely crumbled

Preheat oven to 350°F.

Grease a large baking sheet very well.

Cream the butter with ¾ cup sugar until smooth and fluffy. Beat in the egg yolk, then the flour, lemon juice and zest, and lavender, and mix well to form a soft dough. Place in the refrigerator for 30 minutes. Divide dough into two halves. Working with one half at a time, roll out on a suitable surface until the dough is no more than ¼ inch thick. Cut into shapes—I like cut out circles, half moons, and stars—then place on the baking sheet. Beat the reserved egg white until foamy, then brush lightly onto the cookies with a pastry brush. Sprinkle each cookie with a little of the extra sugar. Bake about 15 minutes or until light golden in color. Cool on a wire rack and repeat with the remaining dough. The cookies keep well stored in an airtight container.

Merrie Yule Liqueur

MAKES APPROXIMATELY 3 CUPS

This simple to make and potent Yuletide libation is full of the spicy, warm flavors we associate with the holidays, and it makes a perfect way to round off a celebratory meal; it's also a wonderful holiday gift. Not only are cinnamon and cloves both warming and healing spices, but cranberries also contain healing properties and lots of vitamin C—very important in the chilly winter months.

Please note that you do need to prepare this liqueur at least a month before you plan on serving it.

> 3 cups good-quality vodka
> ½ cup soft brown sugar
> 1 cinnamon stick
> 2 cloves
> ½ cup raisins
> ¼ cup dried cranberries
> ¼ cup golden raisins

You will need a large glass jar or suitable glass bowl with a lid. Pour the vodka into the jar, then stir in the brown sugar until it is completely dissolved. Add the spices and dried fruits. Cover or seal the jar and keep for at least 1 month in a cool, dark place, stirring the mixture from time to time. Then strain through muslin or coffee filter papers into smaller bottles. If you are giving this as a gift, attach bright, colorful labels and ribbons.

Cranberry Conserve

MAKES ABOUT FOUR ½-PINT JARS

Bright little berries that positively sing with Yuletide energy and goodness—their tangy bite reminds us of their magic powers against negativity and blocked communication on any level. Plus, this conserve just tastes fabulous—not only with roast poultry and other meats, but also with cheese and cold cuts. I never have Brie or Camembert cheese on the table without a little bowl of this conserve alongside.

    1 cup raisins
    ½ cup brown sugar
    1 cup water
    1 small cinnamon stick
    1 teaspoon grated fresh ginger

2 tablespoons lemon juice

2 tablespoons brandy

Grated rind of 1 orange

2 cups fresh cranberries

Combine the raisins, sugar, water, cinnamon stick, and ginger in a saucepan and simmer until the sugar is dissolved. Stir in the lemon juice, brandy, orange rind, and the cranberries, and cook over a low heat until the berries have softened and the mixture is quite thick and syrupy. Take off the heat and remove the cinnamon stick. Spoon into small, sterilized jars. Once opened, keep the conserve in the refrigerator.

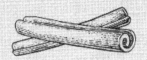

CONCLUSION

As it says so beautifully in the opening quote, recipes are just words on a page until the right person comes along. They need soul, spirit, and magic to make them really happen, and that soul and spirit is you, a kitchen witch, keeper of hearth and home and the sacred flame. A kitchen is a place where we store, prepare, and eat food, yes, but it is also so much more. It can be a sacred place, a place of magic, dreams, and love.

Whoever you are, whatever path you follow, whatever your beliefs may be, I hope this book will be a guide and delicious accompaniment to you in your kitchen during all the magical seasons of the year.

Blessed be … and so it is!

Gail

APPENDIX
Correspondences and Conversions

Each season is linked to one of the four earth elements (fire, air, water, and earth); the fifth element, spirit, is the overriding connection between all that lives and grows on this earth. As such, the seasons carry their own unique energies, which are reflected in the foods and plants linked to them. Creating unique and seasonal meals is a wonderful way of tapping into the wisdom of the earth through all its cycles.

Spring

The Element of Air

This is the season for planting seeds both physically and in the creative and emotional sense: we are moving into new beginnings and plans as we are energized by the bright promise of this blossoming season.

FOODS: yogurt, rice, onions, beans, cheese, peaches, pears, eggs, cherries, grapes, olives, pecans, almonds

HERBS/SPICES: turmeric, mint, parsley, cardamom, oregano, rosemary, coriander, star anise

Summer

The Element of Fire

With its warmth and bright promise, summer is a season to open our hearts and minds to our innate passion and a time to expand our horizons.

FOODS: oranges, carrots, chilies, lamb, corn, grapefruit, beef, chicken, celery, coffee, vinegar

HERBS/SPICES: cayenne pepper, cumin, basil, paprika, saffron, cinnamon, cloves, black pepper, garlic, ginger, bay leaves

Fall

The Element of Water

As the seasons flow and change, so we come to fall, a time of both harvesting and letting go. Water is the symbol of this shift, ever moving and carrying us forward.

FOODS: apples, blackberries, strawberries, cucumber, fish, honey, cabbage, lemons, lettuce, milk, coconut

HERBS/SPICES: thyme, chamomile, lemongrass, salt, vanilla

Winter

The Element of Earth

The quiet time when the earth is cold and frozen, yet still nurturing the promise of spring. It's the time for us to draw inward, too, and nurture ourselves, body and spirit, in a gentle and loving way.

FOODS: potatoes, mushrooms, pumpkin, bread, peanuts, beets, carrots, oats, kale

HERBS/SPICES: marjoram, tarragon, sage

Herb and Spice Correspondences

Since herbs and spices are such an important and magical part of a witch's kitchen, I thought it would be good to include a list of the traditional magical properties and correspondences of the basic herbs and spices used in many of the recipes in this book. Please note, though, that in magical cooking—as in life—everything is open to our individual interpretation; a particular herb or spice may have an entirely different meaning or energy for you, and that's entirely okay. The path of the kitchen witch is a highly individual and personal one, without prescriptive rules or dogma.

ALLSPICE: luck, prosperity, success

BASIL: protection, calming, fidelity, happiness, the removal of unhealthy or harmful patterns in one's life

BAY LEAVES: often used in magical spells and rituals, bay leaves offer courage, wisdom, and the granting of wishes, as well as space clearing and exorcism

BLACK PEPPER: spiritual protection, strength, confidence, warding off evil spirits

CARDAMOM: a warming spice for love, passion, and uplifting the spirit

CAYENNE PEPPER: keeps vampires at bay; for protection of all kinds

CHAMOMILE: calming and relaxing for body and spirit; aids restful sleep

CHIVES: motivates and enhances creativity; a protective herb that helps eliminate bad habits

CILANTRO & CORIANDER SEEDS: creativity, commitment, and positive vibes; also an aphrodisiac and helpful for healing and prosperity spells

CINNAMON: an energetic and healthful spice used for psychic awareness and success rituals

CLOVES: very powerful for removing blocks and negative energies, either for oneself or others; enhances memory and attracts success and abundance

CUMIN: enhances feelings of love and passion; ensures fidelity and loyalty

DILL: a very ancient herb for friendship, love, protection, truthfulness, and removing unwanted ghosts or spirits

Fennel Seed: heals the spirit and creates abundance on every level; also helpful for improving concentration, especially when studying

Garlic: not really an herb but usually included as such, garlic is a powerful protector that repels negative energies, illness, sadness, and mental confusion while protecting the heart and emotions

Ginger: a very enchanted spice used in many magic rituals, ginger gives a boost of courage, energy, and strength to any situation, either physical or emotional, while adding the warmth of passion and protection

Lavender: the most beautiful of herbs, gentle and calming but with a hidden strength; used for spiritual growth, wisdom, peace, and clarity of thought

Lemongrass: perhaps a lesser known herb, although it has been used in the East and in hoodoo ceremonies for many years; invites spirit magic and removes negativity, and lemongrass water can be used for purification and cleansing ceremonies

MARJORAM: loving and uplifting, it can ease the pain of grief, loss, and heartbreak

MINT: for purification, renewal, and moving forward; aids in lucid dreaming, divination, and mental clarity

MUSTARD SEED: for faith, protection, remembrance, and deeper insight into life

NUTMEG: excellent for drawing love towards oneself, attracting love and prosperity, and improving psychic abilities

OREGANO: a happy herb for creating a joyful home and healing past hurts

PAPRIKA: a warming spice that is excellent for magic work of all kinds and creating positive energies

PARSLEY: a herb of purification as well as promoting love and passion; it helps to remove negative entities

ROSE: not really a herb but of tremendous use in the enchanted kitchen for creating feelings of joy, calm, beauty, and love for oneself and others

ROSEMARY: a powerful herb with a multitude of magical uses, especially as regards protection on every level, both physical and emotional; it helps

retain good memories and is also excellent for increasing confidence

SAFFRON: a very happy and energizing spice that works on a deep level to bring us new focus, clarity, and joy

SAGE: the herb of wisdom, it also encourages healing, success, and prosperity, and helps when we are struggling with feelings of anxiety or fear

STAR ANISE: a traditional spice used in many magical rituals for purification, spiritual connection, and the granting of wishes

THYME: this little herb helps to attract the fae and increases psychic awareness and abilities in general; it's also excellent for health and cleansing and brings us renewed willpower and courage

TURMERIC: a traditional spice that has long been used for purification rituals, it helps to banish negative forces of any kind and brings peace to the home

Helpful Kitchen Conversions

Oven Temperatures

Fahrenheit (F)	Celsius (C)	Gas Mark
275	140	1
300	150	2
325	170	3
350	180	4
375	190	5
400	200	6
425	220	7
450	230	8

Measurement Conversions

1 teaspoon	5 ml
1 tablespoon	12.5 ml
¼ cup	60 ml
½ cup	125 ml
¾ cup	200 ml
1 cup	250 ml
3 cups	750 ml
4 cups	1 liter
2 ounces	60 g
4 ounces	125 g
½ pound	250 g
1 pound	500 g
2 pounds	1 kg
1 pint	300 ml
2 pints	1.25 liters

Ingredients

ZUCCHINI: courgette

CILANTRO: coriander (fresh)

CORNSTARCH: cornflour

MOLASSES: treacle

LIGHT CREAM: single cream

HEAVY CREAM: double cream

SCALLIONS: spring onions

CONFECTIONERS' SUGAR: icing sugar

BAKING SODA: bicarbonate of soda

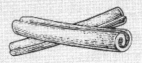

RECOMMENDED READING

This is a short list of my most treasured kitchen witchery books, although not all of them are cookbooks. Some older books may still be found in good secondhand bookstores or at online retailers.

Alink, Merissa A. *Little House Living*. New York: Gallery Books, 2015. A guide for living your life simply and frugally, with lots of kitchen and home ideas for the down-to-earth kitchen witch.

Bradley, Kris. *Mrs B's Guide to Household Witchery*. San Francisco: Weiser Books, 2012. A simply delightful and accessible book about living the green witchy life!

Bussi, Gail. *Bake Happy!* Cape Town: Random House Struik, 2014. This was my first cookbook, full of my favorite baking recipes and lots of memories.

Gaston, Meredith. *Find Your Sparkle*. Melbourne, Australia: Hardie Grant Books, 2019. This is a lovely illustrated book about creating individual well-being on every level, written by a talented author and artist; it also has lots of ideas for interesting vegan recipes.

Glenn, Camille. *The Heritage of Southern Cooking*. New York: Workman, 1995. Another favorite filled with the tastes and flavors of the South.

Johnson, Cait. *Witch in the Kitchen*. Rochester, VT: Destiny Books, 2001. This is one of my favorite books of kitchen magic, and I love its seasonal ideas and recipes.

Kempton, Beth. *Wabi Sabi, Japanese Wisdom for a Perfectly Imperfect Life*. London, UK: Piatkus, 2018. Traditional wisdom for finding joy and meaning in the simple things of life.

Kindred, Glennie. *The Alchemist's Journey*. London, UK: Hay House, 2005. A beautiful and insightful account of following the wheel of the Celtic year and its personal impact on the author.

McBride, Kami. *The Herbal Kitchen*. Newburyport, MA: Conari Press, 2019. A great resource for herbal pantry and stillroom ideas.

Murphy-Hiscock, Arin. *The Way of the Hedge Witch*. Avon, MA: Adams Media, 2009. A good and practical introduction to the life and magic of a hedge witch.

Nickerson, Brittany Wood. *Recipes from an Herbalist's Kitchen*. North Adams, MA: Storey, 2016. My favorite book about using herbs in the kitchen and beyond for nutrition, health, and healing.

Patterson, Rachel. *A Kitchen Witch's World of Magical Food*. Winchester, UK: Moon Books, 2015. A down-to-earth guide showing how cooking can be a truly magical art.

Rombauer, Irma S., and Marion Rombauer Becker. *The Joy of Cooking*. New York: Penguin Putnam, 1999. This is, of course, a definitive kitchen book, and I turn to it again and again for practical kitchen insights and information.

Shababy, Doreen. *The Wild and Weedy Apothecary*. Woodbury, MN: Llewellyn, 2010. Another great natural cooking and healing resource, written in a charming and accessible style.

Valentine, Radleigh. *Compendium of Magical Things*. Carlsbad, CA: Hay House, 2018. A charming book showing us different ways of accessing magic and spirit through different practices like tarot, meditation, astrology, and the enchantment of angels and faery.

Watson Hopping, Jane. *The Pioneer Lady's Country Christmas* (New York: Villard Books, 1989) and *Lazy Days of Summer Cookbook* (New York: Villard Books, 1992). These are wonderfully old-fashioned, charming cookbooks loaded with lots of down to earth (and affordable) recipes.

Whitehurst, Tess. *Magical Housekeeping*. Woodbury, MN: Llewellyn, 2010. A great resource for keeping your home happy, healthy, and full of magic energy!

To Write to the Author

If you wish to contact the author or would like more information about this book, please write to the author in care of Llewellyn Worldwide and we will forward your request. Both the author and the publisher appreciate hearing from you and learning of your enjoyment of this book and how it has helped you. Llewellyn Worldwide cannot guarantee that every letter written to the author can be answered, but all will be forwarded. Please write to:

Gail Bussi
℅ Llewellyn Worldwide
2143 Woodedale Drive
Woodbury, MN 55125-2989

Please enclose a self-addressed stamped envelope for reply or $1.00 to cover costs. If outside the USA, enclose an international postal reply coupon.

Many of Llewellyn's authors have websites with additional information and resources. For more information, please visit our website:

WWW.LLEWELLYN.COM